MARLEY DIAS
IN THE SPOTLIGHT

FEATURED SPEAKER, THE WHITE HOUSE,
UNITED STATE OF WOMEN SUMMIT

SELECTED BY TEEN VOGUE AMONG THE
"10 AMAZING BLACK WOMEN WHO ARE CHANGING
THE GAME"

NAMED "COOLEST BLACK KID IN AMERICA"
BY *EBONY* MAGAZINE

CHOSEN FOR GLAMOUR.COM'S LIST OF
"THE BEST GIRL-POWERED MOMENTS . . .
ACCORDING TO MALALA"

FEATURED AMONG LITERARY HUB'S
"THE BIGGEST LITERARY STORIES OF THE YEAR . . ."

INCLUDED IN MTV.COM'S
"12 SOCIAL MEDIA WARRIORS WHO HELPED
RESTORE OUR FAITH . . ."

HIGHLIGHTED ON THE BLACK WOMEN IN HISTORY
TUMBLR'S LIST OF "10 BLACK KIDS WHO
ROCKED THE WORLD . . ."

MARLEY DIAS
gets it
DONE

AND SO CAN YOU!

by **MARLEY DIAS**

with *Siobhan McGowan*

Introduction by Ava DuVernay

SCHOLASTIC PRESS | NEW YORK

Library of Congress Cataloging-in-Publication Data available

ISBN 978-1-338-13689-0

10 9 8 7 6 5 4 3 2 1   18 19 20 21 22

Printed in the U.S.A. 40

First edition, February 2018

Book design by Mary Claire Cruz and Abby Dening

To Mommy and Daddy and SuperGirls everywhere —M.D.

CONTENTS

Introduction

BY AVA DUVERNAY

I first met Marley Dias on a sunny day in New Orleans. She was eleven years old then, a beautiful brew of kindness, confidence, and curiosity. We sat and talked about books and bravery. How books have allowed us both to experience bold adventures in our imagination. How bravery has led us to experience bold adventures in our real lives.

The author and cultural icon Helen Keller once wrote: "Life is either a daring adventure or nothing. To keep our faces toward change and behave like free spirits in the presence of fate is strength undefeatable." These words describe Marley Dias in a nutshell. A free spirit rooted in strength. A daring adventurer unafraid to challenge the status quo and build her dreams into reality.

In your hands, you hold a beautiful book powered by sheer determination. In the very title, *Marley Dias Gets It Done*, you can feel her drive. A drive that led a young girl to shape a movement called #1000blackgirlbooks as remedy for what she didn't see. A drive that epitomizes the key to success. It is simply this: Embrace passion for your ideas and do not let it go. Period. Every success story has this rule at its heart. Marley's included. Enjoy her gem of a book, and revel in her example of cultivating passion into the realization of dreams. Then, dare to do the same for yourself. A great adventure awaits you.

Prologue
DO SOMETHING

Writing a book is fun, hard, and scary. But what's even scarier is seeing an injustice that you want to change and feeling like there is nothing you can do about it.

Through this experience, I have learned that the best way to end that scary feeling is to actually do something. And that's one of the main reasons I've written this book. I was afraid that if I did nothing, things would just stay the way they are. And I didn't like where things were headed. I had been taught to value diversity as well as my own culture, and yet every required reading list I ever got in school didn't have books that featured black girls as the main characters. That's why (semi-spoiler alert) over a pancake breakfast with my mom—who encouraged me to stop whining and to do something—I came up with the idea to launch a campaign to collect a thousand books featuring black girls as lead protagonists. I never could have imagined what has happened since. And that's been the hard part. My #1000blackgirlbooks campaign showed me that it is impossible to just witness injustice and do nothing. It's hard to stand still when there is so much to be done. I'm excited to do something and to show you that you can too.

I soon realized that as someone who loves to read and someone who finds guidance and motivation in books, it was time for me to share some of what I've learned about social action. This book is my opportunity to give and share what I am learning and have learned. During my travels, I have met thousands of kids like me who are passionate about their own causes, who have dreams they want to make come true, and who are ready to do something. I'm eager to share my story with them and with you. When it comes to social action, like participating in marches and demonstrations, most of what I convey and suggest is based on my own experiences. Other examples come from my observations and interactions with kids like me who are passionate about causes they believe in.

I hope these words will motivate others, as well as open conversations about how young people can change things, with the help of trusted and loving adults.

Grown-ups, parents, teachers, and caregivers, please pay attention! The kids you know and love may be young, but we can stretch ourselves to be wiser than our years in many ways—through our ideas, with the help of social media—and we can make a difference with your help.

In this book, I'm excited to introduce you to me and my family, to welcome you to my world, and to give you an up-close-and-personal, step-by-step account of how my campaign went from a small grassroots movement to something much bigger.

But this book isn't a memoir or a self-help book. (I've never liked being put into a category.) It's not a memoir because, though I let you in on my life, this book isn't about me; it's about what we can do together.

To see what I mean, do me a favor . . . read this book's title slowly, and let your eyes linger on the very last word: You! That's the really important part of my story—how you, with some help from me and others, can get lots of things done when everyone is on the same page.

Marley Dias Gets It Done: And So Can You! is my wish for a better tomorrow. It's my invitation to anyone who reads this book to do something about anything that doesn't feel right to you. Use your frustrations to guide you to make a difference in the world. I'm also telling my story because I need your help in making important changes. Please share this book with others and use it to dream big and achieve goals that will help us create a more inclusive and diverse world.

That's the fun part. When you dive into these pages, you can dream really big and achieve even higher.

You can think about things that don't seem right in your world and brainstorm ways to improve them.

You can gather your friends and anyone who loves and supports you and work together.

You can take something tiny and turn it into something timeless. To me, that's what activism is—forging a path that will: 1) give others something meaningful to follow 2) blaze a trail that can't ever be turned back and 3) offer a road map to make the course easier for others (because great work is never done). Please help me by using my book as a guide so that we can get it done together.

I hope that when you read this book—or any book at all—it will feel like you are giving yourself a gift that you're excited to share.

I have had lots of people ask me, "Marley, who's this book for?"

Here's what I tell them:

Just because I'm a teenager doesn't mean you have to be a kid to use these tools that come from my experience. This book is for anyone who cares deeply about the world. If you're a kid like me, show this book to anyone who's old enough to vote.

Also (and I know this sounds silly, but . . .), you don't have to be a black girl to find value in what I've got to say. *Marley Dias Gets It Done: And So Can You!* is for everyone.

A final word about something I've learned from being on this awesome journey: There's more to a book than just reading it. This one, especially, requires certain things to make it the best it can be for you, and for our future.

WHAT YOU NEED TO READ *THIS* BOOK IS . . .

- Any dream worth following
- A strong belief in something (preferably yourself and your community)
- A right-sized ego (no room for divas when it comes to activism)
- Patience
- Curiosity
- People who love you and trusted adults who want to help you succeed

It's time to do something amazing!

Marley Dias

Herstory

WHO I AM, HOW THIS ALL BEGAN

1

Herstory

WHO I AM,
HOW THIS ALL BEGAN

If only there'd been one book at school . . . just one . . . about a black girl and her dog . . .

A brainiac black girl astronaut with her trailblazing space poodle, exploring the rings of Saturn . . .

A fierce black girl fashion designer with her frisky Rottweiler on a rhinestone leash, owning the streets of the city . . .

A fearless black girl forensic archaeologist with her inquisitive collie, uncovering the fossil remains of some prehistoric species . . .

If only, then maybe none of this would have happened. I wouldn't be such a public advocate for black girl books. I wouldn't have had to write this book. I'd just be your typical girl in a New Jersey public school, checking off the titles on her assigned reading list, cramming for tests, playing video games with my best friend, and binge-watching slime and cat videos on YouTube.

Maybe.

But then again, I doubt it.

And that's not what happened anyway.

And I'm not that average girl. I'm Marley Emerson Dias.

"Use what you have to make the world a better place in your own way." —MARLEY DIAS, UNITED STATE OF WOMEN SUMMIT

I'm a teenager. And I'm an activist. For literacy. For diversity. For equity and positive social change. And you can be too! You may think we're too young to have any influence on or make a real difference in this so often messed-up world, but I'm proof we're not. Because I already did it, I'm going to keep on doing it, and so can you. I'll help by telling you how.

But hold up. Wait a minute, Marley, slow down. I'm getting ahead of myself, as usual. Thinking out loud, as fast as I talk (and if you've ever heard me talk, you know). First, let me tell you what *did* happen.

Me and Mom at The Ellen DeGeneres Show.

It all began, as a matter of fact, over a plate of pancakes.

Mmmm, pancakes . . .

THE POWER OF PANCAKES

Pancakes are the definition of awesome, don't you agree? Look it up in the dictionary if you don't believe me. Breakfast in general is the best. My mom thinks so too. We pretty much eat breakfast at all hours of the day. We have breakfast for dinner if we so choose. Sometimes at home, sometimes at diners—New Jersey being the unofficial diner capital of the world, of course.

So my mom and I were snug in a booth at a diner one Thursday after school. Or maybe it was a Tuesday. And I was eating pancakes, all good. It was November, almost the holidays. We were talking, just about stuff: the year that was coming to an end, the year that was about to begin. My mom, who is brilliant and the coolest and completely crazy— I'm not being a brat, anyone in my family would say the same,

Bestselling authors Jacqueline Woodson (left), me, and Rita Williams-Garcia.

but more on her later—my mom asked me:

"If you could change one thing in the new year, Marley, what would it be?"

Hmmm.

Good question, Mom!

I took a long moment to consider it, hand-cupping-chin-contemplative-smiley-emoji style, and then it came to me.

BLACK GIRL READING

Some background info: Not long before this pancake convo, I had (finally) finished a ridiculously amazing book. A book the likes of which I had never read before. Instead of chapters, there were time periods. Instead of paragraphs, there were poems. Some poems were three pages long. Others were four lines short. But they all were super descriptive, bringing to mind everything from the glow of fireflies in summer, to the cryptic graffiti scribbled on city buildings, to that nervous-excited feeling you get on the first day of first grade—I mean everything, really. The story was autobiographical. And the main character—the protagonist—was a black girl. A black girl like me. Except she had grown up in the 1960s and '70s, during the civil rights movement, in Brooklyn and the Jim Crow South.

My titi—that's a Spanish word for "auntie"—my titi Eva had given me the book *Brown Girl Dreaming* by Jaqueline Woodson as a birthday gift when I was nine years old. In my family, we give books as gifts all the time. To be honest, I am a tbn: total book nerd. I devour them—flipping through their pages as fast as I think and talk. But *Brown Girl Dreaming* was different. At nine, I just didn't get it. At all. The poetry. The lack of the usual plot. All that pretty imagery—what did it mean? For the first time ever, I set a book aside. Put it back on the shelf in my bedroom. When my aunt asked me, a whole year later, how I'd liked it, I

had to admit to her that—shocker in the DiasCrew—I hadn't read it; it was too hard to understand.

"Maybe," she challenged me gently, "you should try again."

(Can you tell by now that all the women in my family are completely boss?)

Anyway, I did try again, and with the benefit of age, patience, and maturity, ha-ha, suddenly Jacqueline Woodson's story-in-verse made complete sense to me. No, it more than made sense; it opened a whole new world to me. A world where modern black girls were the

Mom is always by my side.

> *"[Marley] is my dream twenty-first-century person, in terms of realizing something needs to be changed and making it happen."* —JACQUELINE WOODSON

main characters—not invisible, not just the sidekick. A world where black girls were free to be complicated, honest, human; to have adventures and emotions unique just to them. A world where black girls' stories truly mattered. And it was *beautiful*.

Because that was not exactly the world I was experiencing in real life, back in fifth grade. In my class—in all the fifth-grade classes—we were required to read "classics": books like *Shiloh*, which is about a white boy and the dog he rescues. And *Old Yeller*, which is about a white boy and the dog that rescues him. And *Where the Red Fern Grows*, which is about a white boy and the *two* dogs he

trains. These were all good stories. Not to be disrespectful about any white people, dogs, or any of those books, or their authors—and I know lots of kids love books like those—but I mean, seriously! One of them had been awarded the Newbery Honor and another the Newbery Medal. But so had many black authors. It's like winning an Oscar for your book; if you win it, you are basically officially one of the best authors on the planet. We could have had other options. What about *Brown Girl Dreaming* and *One Crazy Summer* by Rita Williams-Garcia?

There were students of all different races and ethnicities in my class. Just not in the books we were

assigned to read. And no black authors had written any book on our reading lists.

Which brings me back to the diner. And that question my mom posed over pancakes, about what I would change if I could. I gulped down a mouthful of fluffy, yummy, flapjacky goodness, then answered her.

"I'd make it so that kids in my class, in my grade—that kids being included, of our stories not being told." And I was. "I am *sooo* sick and tired of reading books about white boys and their dogs!"

Roll of Thunder, Hear My Cry by Mildred D. Taylor won the 1977 Newbery Medal. It had been around a long time like those other books. Why wasn't it considered a classic? *Brown Girl Dreaming* has also won a Newbery Honor Medal, the Coretta Scott King Award,

> *"I don't look up to any specific person. I find qualities in people that I admire. No one is perfect and I don't think saying that I aspire to be one person is the best idea because it puts pressure on you to have [a] specific goal."* —MARLEY DIAS, BLAVITY.COM

everywhere—could read books with black girls as the main characters," I said. "Books like *Brown Girl Dreaming*. I'm tired of us not the NAACP Image Award, and the National Book Award. *One Crazy Summer* has also won most of these awards, too. That's like

sweeping the Oscars in every category. Why wasn't it considered a classic too? Why wasn't it mandatory reading?

My mom gave me a look across the table. That way she does when she's going to drop some truth.

"Well," she replied, "that's an interesting dilemma, Marley. What are you going to do about it?"

I repeat: Good question, Mom!

WHAT DIFFERENCE DOES IT MAKE?

I didn't know it at the time—I was just articulating my own personal frustration—but I had run smack up against an issue that affects millions of students, both in America and around the world. I would later learn that fewer than 10 percent of children's books published in 2015 featured a black person as the main character. And that's a problem. Frankly, it's unfair.

Don't get me wrong: I was already reading books with black girl protagonists. At home. But the only books we'd read at school were slave narratives set in the eighteenth and nineteenth centuries or stories with stressed-out girls from the civil rights movement. While these stories are extremely important because they portray the strength and resilience of black girls throughout history, they can get depressing and disappointing when it's all that schools offer. The range of black girl experiences is so much broader, and deeper, and richer than that!

There's an expression: "How can you be it if you can't see it?" Meaning, if the examples of black characters—black astronauts and fashion designers and forensic archaeologists and tech entrepreneurs and ballet dancers and movie directors and presidents of the United States—don't exist in fiction or in the movies or on TV, then how would we even know it was a possibility, an option, to be any of those things ourselves?

I understand that logic, I do. And it may be true for many people, although I myself don't 100 percent accept it. I believe in the power of our imagination and intelligence to create something where there was nothing before, to manifest it, with the encouragement of our family and our community, and with inspiration from whoever's come before. That's what creativity, and originality are all about. After all, there hadn't been a black president before Barack

BROWN GIRL DREAMING, by Jacqueline Woodson, changed my life. It was the first book that ever challenged me as a reader—I had to put it down and not pick it up again for a whole year before it really made sense to me. The experience of going from not understanding to understanding taught me that time can solve a lot of problems. It taught me patience. It even humbled me a bit!

> **"Seeing a story on a page about a black child written by a black author . . . legitimizes your own existence in the world, because you're a part of something else. 'Look, I'm here in this book.'"** —JACQUELINE WOODSON

Obama. There had been civil rights leaders and senators and professors, but not a president. Until—boom!—Barack Obama happened, and then there was. (And with Barack came Michelle Obama, the one and only black first lady, and Sasha and Malia, the first African American president's children.) Now these barriers can never be unbroken. In other words, there has to be a first, a pioneer, to set the example. A person who envisions the possibilities even when she can't literally see them, and who then goes on to embody them. Yay!

If representation isn't an absolute necessity, though, that doesn't mean it's not majorly important. Or deserved. Or that it doesn't make a difference. Lots of books offer important lessons about how to deal with complicated issues. But if the characters don't reflect you, if you can't relate to them, it can be more difficult to absorb the morals of the stories. They may make less of an impact and leave less of an imprint on your heart, mind, and soul. You'll close the covers of the book, with its lessons still buried.

Not every girl is lucky enough

to be raised in a smart, support-ive family and community like I've been. Those girls especially need the power of example in the books they read, because they may not see it anywhere else in their world. Without representa-tion, they risk losing their sense of identity—if they ever even had it in the first place.

Sad.

Beyond sad.

Wrong.

Plus, to get basic about it:

How can educators expect kids to love, instead of dread, reading when they never see themselves in the stories they're forced to read? Since most kids have to go to school, being in class every day can be a way to give kids hope—or the opposite, if a teacher or school doesn't see that all kinds of books and experiences are important. If there are no black girl books as part of the school curriculum, then how are we expected to believe all that stuff that teachers

and parents are constantly telling us about how we're "all equal"? If we're all equal, then we should all be represented equally. If black girls' stories are missing, then the implication is that they don't matter. I didn't like it so I had to do something.

A HASHTAG IS BORN

But what was I going to do? Fortunately, thanks in part to my involvement in GrassROOTS Community Foundation's girls' camp, which teaches confidence and social activism (more on that later too), I had a few thoughts on the subject. Over pancakes and juice that afternoon, I came up with an idea: I would collect books, of course. Lots of them. I would get donations of not 100, not 500, but, because it seemed like an appropriately huge number, 1,000 books featuring black girls as the main characters. I'd get 1,000 books, and I'd give them away wherever they were needed most, and soon everybody would be reading about awesome us.

My goal was to do this by February—and it was November.

How I was going to do it, I had no idea. Where were the books going to come from? Not a clue. All I knew was that this—the importance of including black girl voices—was my truth. My passion. I had to make it happen. Somehow. Even if it had never been done before.

A hashtag.

That was the way to start.

A hashtag, because if there's one thing I'd learned from watching slime and cat videos on YouTube, social media is powerful.

It is also, however, full of tons of cyber junk that almost nobody ever sees. And, if you're a kid, there are risks involved in using social media. It has to be done responsibly and should always involve the guidance of your parents (check

out Chapter 5 for some super-important info on social media dos and don'ts).

My biggest challenge in going viral was to come up with something fun, catchy. Unforgettable.

Yes! A hashtag was born.

#1000BlackGirlBooks

My mom posted the hashtag first and her friends also used it, because at that time I did not have my own social media account.

As for what happened next and how I started a movement, well, read on.

Meet My Family

WELCOME TO MY VILLAGE

2

Meet My Family

WELCOME TO MY VILLAGE

MY AMAZING MOM

How many times have I heard people say, "the apple doesn't fall far from the tree"? In Jamaica, the elders say, "*Chip nuh fall far from di tree.*" That means kids tend to follow in their parents' footsteps. Whether it's an apple or a chip, both expressions are used by older people. And both are true.

Even though we wear different shoes sizes (I'm a 10, Mom's an 11), and have different tastes in footwear (as you see on the cover of this book, I can wear a pair of gold leathers; Mom's more of a traditional-sneaker type), my mom and I walk the same walk—together. We're in step most of the time because we both believe in helping others, and we're both doing what it takes to keep girls healthy, strong, and confident. I have learned the value of service from Mom, who, from *her* mom, got the same message very early in life. So I guess you could say that "paying it forward" (another term older people use, but that works for me) is my family tradition. Helping people is a family inheritance. I've also been taught that

> **"My parents are always pushing me to do my best, even though my best may not be like other people's bests."** –MARLEY DIAS

anything worth keeping strong must be shared, or it gets weak really fast.

My mom, Dr. Janice Johnson Dias, is Jamaican. She grew up in Retreat, St. Mary, Jamaica, one of the most beautiful places on the planet. Did you know that Jamaica has the highest percentage of women managers in the world? It's true! Can you imagine being raised in a place like that? An island-country where you see women running the government, making positive changes, and speaking up and out. Imagine having women's achievement

SOMETIMES PARENTS JUST DON'T UNDERSTAND

OK, just between you and me, even though my parents are amazing, and I love them, we can butt heads when Mom *and* Dad join forces and boss me around.

Like all parents, mine have rules. Mom and Dad are strict about sports. They insist that I play a sport every season because they've read a bunch of studies about how important physical health is to a teenager's mental health. My parents are always the first to tell anyone who will listen that sports are good for cutting down on stress and building self-confidence. I agree with all that. I used to play lacrosse, I was the quarterback for my football team (Dad volunteered to be our team coach), and I played basketball when I was little. After a day on the field or court, I felt powerful, and I've discovered that it's somehow easier to get homework done after I've worked out. My mind is sharp and ready to learn. At the same time, sports definitely bring on the calm, which I've noticed after a practice or a game.

But here's where Mom and Dad and me sort of clash. It's about attitude. Why do my parents have to be the leading authorities on everything, carrying on about all the studies they've read that say how sports supposedly make teens better people? Even though they're right about athletics and how good they are for you, it bugs me that they feel they have to remind me of it all the time.

On top of that, Mom and Dad and I can really have our moments when it comes to what they think is "appropriate" for kids my age. They check everything I read to make sure there's nothing "bad" in the books I pick. And *they're* the ones who decide what's considered "bad," even when I try to convince them that their version of "bad" is not the same as mine.

Mom and Dad do the same thing with music. I was born in West Philly, where the old TV show *The Fresh Prince of Bel-Air* takes place. It stars Will Smith, who recorded a song called "Parents Just Don't Understand" with DJ Jazzy Jeff. "Parents Just Don't Understand" was often mentioned on episodes of the show, and every time that happened, I shouted "Yes!" at the TV.

The truth is, parents want to protect kids, but when moms and dads try too hard to keep us from "bad" stuff, sometimes they miss opportunities to teach us "good" stuff and lessons we can use. And sometimes they miss opportunities to learn from us. Parents can underestimate our ability to understand and evaluate the meaning of things happening in the world, whether they're depicted in books or in songs.

When it comes to music, I hear it all the time from my parents. They *loooove* to preach about how today's music is just not as good as music from "back in the day." Whenever they come on with this, I want to say, "Oh, please, not that song again!" At any time, my mom or dad will subject me to every late '80s and early '90s song that they can find on YouTube. They say they want to introduce me to a time when music was "good."

I've had to listen to Anita Baker, Tracy Chapman, Gladys Knight, and Lauryn Hill over and over again. I've now watched the Janet and Michael Jackson "Scream" video at least ten times. While I admit that Janet and Michael are really good together, I don't need to watch that video again, thank you very much.

The rapper JAY-Z is one of the bestselling musicians of all time.

My parents also make me listen to every '80s and '90s rapper in the world. My dad even quotes rappers when he talks in a regular conversation. I think his goal is to make it sound like the raps are his words, when, in reality they belong to Biggie, Rakim, Nas, and other rappers.

Whether it's '80s, '90s, or today's music, my folks, like other parents, are always quick to edit the music that I like. My dad controls the music I listen to by talking loudly during the places in songs where there's profanity. My mom is even more strict than my dad. She will fast-forward or change the song. Sometimes she even says "OH MY GROSSNESS!"

when some songs come on. I know they think they're protecting me, but what they're really doing is ruining the songs I like!

The fact is, I can hear more "bad" stuff during the day at school, on the bus, and on TV—more than I will ever hear on the radio during a fifteen-minute car ride, or over breakfast, while the music plays.

To me, music is transformative and educational. My parents clearly know the power of music. My mom dances with me all the time. And because my dad DJs on the side, he's all about the rhythms. But I don't think my parents truly understand what music means to me, deep down.

My parents are not alone in this. I think most parents don't understand what music means to their kids, and how listening to music and reading share some of the same advantages.

Like books, music offers the ability to connect with ideas, to get insights about the world, and to explore new ways of thinking. Music, and the stories we read, free us to imagine. They open our hearts, clear our minds. Music, reading, and writing transport us to different places.

In my opinion, just because there's a "bad" word or two in a book or a song, that doesn't make the whole thing "bad."

As kids, we're dealing with a lot of issues. When a good book dives into these issues, or when a song comes on the radio, or television, or Pandora, or YouTube, it's a great chance for parents to talk to us about their values—and ours.

"Bad" is an opportunity to learn. When parents snatch a book away, or lower the volume, or change the music, they're cutting off a way they can connect with us. They are turning down our voices.

But hey, I want to be clear about something. Parents are looking out for their kids. I get that. To help my own parents understand me better, I talk to them. A lot. Maybe sometimes too much. I let my mom and dad know why I like certain books, music, authors, and recording artists, and anything else we may view differently. How can parents understand us if we don't help them see things through our eyes? So, when your mom or dad doesn't see your point of view, have a sit-down. Talk to one another. You may not come to an eye-to-eye agreement, but at least there's a conversation happening. This is a way to let our voices be turned back up a bit, to be heard, and it's a chance to hear where Mom and Dad are coming from.

inspirations for starting my book drive. Soon after we realized that #1000blackgirlbooks had collected well over a thousand titles, Mom and I immediately chose to donate 1,000 books to where my mom, grandma, and great-grandma went to school, and we also donated 700 books to her hometown's library.

I love to hear people call my mom "Dr. Janice." Mom's got a PhD in sociology, which means she's an expert in understanding how systems affect how people behave in groups. That's a great thing to know when you're working hard to make positive changes that affect entire communities.

considered normal. Add to that, the fact that Jamaica is a tropical paradise, and you've got one fantastic place to enjoy your childhood.

At the same time, though, like every nation on the planet, Jamaica has some impoverished places, and so there is a shortage of books for kids in many parts of the country. My mom grew up in one of the communities that lacked books. The library in my mom's hometown was not open very often when she was a kid. She primarily had access only to the Bible. This lack of reading material was one of the

> *"I've dedicated my life to bridging the gap between the so-called thinkers and the doers."*
> —DR. JANICE JOHNSON DIAS

Mom and me at a GrassROOTs event.

Mom is the president of the GrassROOTS Community Foundation, an organization created to build a world where *all* girls grow up to be healthy women. (See the sidebar on page 45 to learn more about my mom's brilliant brainchild.)

People always want to know if Mom and I ever disagree. What do you think? Of course we do! And often.

Since I was a little kid, Mom has laid down some pretty solid and serious ground rules around my bedtime. Its sounds strict, but Mom operates under the belief that a kid under eleven needs eleven hours of sleep each night to be at her best. Sometimes I'm just not tired, or I'd rather stay up late to finish making slime or doing homework. But I'll admit, getting lots of time under the covers helps me stay focused and strong during the day.

Another area where Mom and I can disagree a lot is over how to phrase or say something. I'm a teenager, and I have *my* ways of

LIFE LESSONS MOM AND DAD HAVE TAUGHT ME

Both my parents come from military backgrounds, and I'm thankful for that. They truly understand the importance of having a routine , and sticking with it. They also value serving others through compassionate social action. Here's a snapshot of life lessons that I keep in mind at all times.

In every interaction, practice the 3 Cs: courtesy, communication, commitment

• COURTESY: Say hello, look people in the eye, and give a strong handshake or loving hug.
• COMMUNICATION: Be clear and don't mumble your words.
• COMMITMENT: Be true to your word; if you say you are going to do something, then do it.
• COMMUNITY MATTERS: Don't go it alone. I never could've started my book collection without the guidance of my family and friends. Call on people who share your passions and let them help.
• BE CALM AND CLEAR: Think before speaking. Simple, but not always easy.
• INTEGRITY MATTERS: Be you, 'cause you're the only you you've got.
• BEING HEALTHY FEELS GOOD: Eat well. Sleep well. And laugh a lot.

expressing *my* ideas to speak to kids *my* age. Mom's a mother, and she has *her* ways of expressing *her* ideas to people *her* age. What's cool about this is that we're often saying the exact same things, but expressing them differently. That's part of where the apple and the chip aren't too far from the mother tree, which is totally fine with me. The closer Mom and I stick together, the more I know she's always got my back.

Things can get hairy, though, when she *and* my dad come together and lay down the law, especially on certain issues. (Check out my take on this in "Sometimes Parents Just Don't Understand" on page 36). But first, meet . . .

MY AWESOME DAD

I've gotta hand it to my father. He's outnumbered in our household. He is the only guy living with me and my mom, two headstrong people who are all about women's and girls' empowerment.

But my father, Scott Dias, is one of the most active feminists

"A lot of Marley's success comes from watching her mother, and her mom's ability to balance life, friends, and her work." —SCOTT DIAS

I know. It's one thing for a man to *say* he believes in supporting causes that benefit women and girls, but it's a whole other thing for a man to put his beliefs into action by *doing*.

Dad is a real estate analytical geographer. Whew, that's a big title, right? It means Dad helps businesses find locations to build new stores in parts of town that can keep the businesses growing and benefit the communities they serve.

My father's passion for the natural environment, and how it affects humans and the ways and places people live, makes him the perfect person to be my mom's husband and my father. His job is so closely linked to what Mom and I are striving for—connecting people to resources, helping them feel safe and grounded wherever they live, and making the world a better place.

My dad was born in Hyannis, Massachusetts, but his family on both sides are from Cape Verde, a set of islands off the coast of Senegal. He comes from a proud, strong family that believes in the importance of sticking together. Dad grew up with the belief that

GrassROOTS
Community Foundation

MY GRASSROOTS VILLAGE

Thank goodness for roots. Mine run deep. A couple of years ago, my mom started GrassROOTS Community Foundation (GCF), a public health and social action organization to help women and girls make their lives, families, and communities strong. GCF does some of the most amazing things. Aside from helping to get #1000blackgirlbooks going, GCF is making this planet better by:

• Developing health and wellness programs for women and girls, particularly those who are impoverished.

• Training young girls to use their skills and talents to make a difference in the world.

• Guiding and mentoring black girls all over the world.

• Advocating for policies and practices that foster equity.

• Providing technical support to health and community programs.

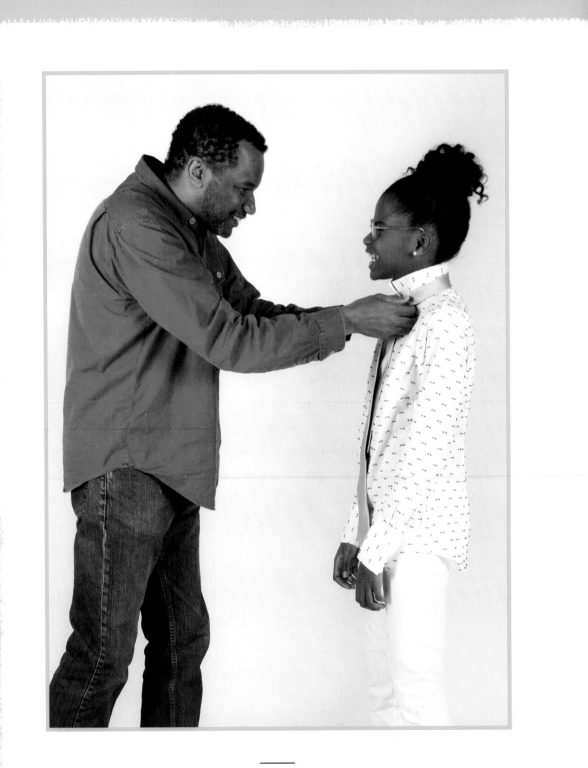

men and women are meant to be equal partners. Mom says he's a cross between John "Grizzly" Adams, a famous mountain man who saved and adopted a grizzly bear and found comfort with animals (and became the subject of a popular TV series from when my parents were kids), and

MacGyver, a former military guy who always gets himself out of dangerous scrapes using gadgets and brainpower on another oldie television show (now a remake on CBS). MacGyver served in the US Army as a bomb team technician and my dad was a combat engineer for six years in the United States Army Reserves.

Since I don't watch those shows, here's how I see it. If my dad and mom were a car, Mom would be the engine, and Dad would be the battery that keeps the motor running. We can't drive our #1000blackgirlbooks mission or GrassROOTS Community Foundation—and even our home—without my dad!

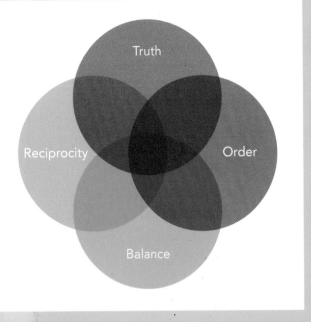

THE PRINCIPLE OF TRUTH

At GrassROOTS, that's the first thing we learn. We're taught how to tell facts from myths, and how to speak truth to power. We learn the value of honesty and the importance of doing right even when no one is watching. We focus on being our best selves.

Truth is the first of four principles we learn about and have to follow at SuperCamp. The remaining three are Order, Balance, and Reciprocity. All four are elements of Maat, the concept of justice that was developed in ancient Kemet (now called Egypt) by African people more than 2,000 years ago. There was a goddess who carried a feather and who had the same name. The ancient Egyptians believed she ruled the stars, the seasons—the entire universe, basically. Maat kept everything from falling into chaos, and she made sure her spirit was as light as a feather. In other words, even though she was dealing with serious issues, she also kept things easygoing. Maat was a real shero.

The principle of Order is about respecting time; recognizing that there is a time and a place for everything. Time reaches back into our history, embracing generations, so we also show respect for those who came before us; they are our ancestors—both blood relatives and the elders in our community. We honor their experiences and gratefully receive the wisdom they share.

The principle of Balance teaches us to use our energy and resources wisely in everyday life.

We work to keep things in perspective and not push ourselves so hard or stretch ourselves so thin that we burn out. When we achieve balance, we are able to study hard, but also find time for rest and relaxation. Celebrating with friends at a birthday party, concert, or dance can be fun, but time by yourself in peace and quiet can also feel just as good. These are only a couple of illustrations of Balance.

Reciprocity is my favorite principle (along with Truth): It's about giving back. When we reciprocate, we share the best within ourselves with the rest of the world. But we're not just doing the world a favor; we're making it a better place. And when the world's better, everybody's happier—including me and you. Now, I am not saying we participate in Reciprocity simply for our own sake. It's about how we're all connected. Since all actions have effects, we choose to make ours positive. Good vibes only, as the saying goes!

By following these four principles, I have grown more confident and capable of using my talents for the benefit of my family and my community. If you put the effort into learning about yourself, they'll click for you too, around something you love, something that matters deeply to you. For me, it was reading. When I realized there was a lack of diversity in the literature we were assigned at school, I was motivated to launch my campaign. Because reading has given me so much, I was inspired to give back—to reciprocate. #1000blackgirlbooks and the need to include black girl voices in our cultural conversation are *my* truth. What's yours?

To explore, check out the GCF website. You'll also see why Mom is my shero!

grassrootscommunityfoundation.org

My dad has taught me a lot about fishing.

At school, I'm in honors math and science. I like it a lot and I get to learn tons of new things about the natural world. My dad's the same way. I get my math-science interest from him. Dad has a degree in geology from the Department of Earth and Atmospheric Science, City College of New York. When I was little, Dad and I loved making structures of blocks and playing with worms. Now that I'm older, we make slime together.

If you give Dad a tech challenge, he can solve it. I'm the same way. When my hashtag started picking up steam, my dad helped me manage all the tech involved. And my father loves to DJ! He is really good. He spins at all the GrassROOTS events and at my birthday parties. He loves to show me how it's done. He taught me how to DJ. I am not as good as him yet, but I soon will be, and maybe even better.

Dad is a really serious fisherman. He's taught me everything I know about catching a big one. We fish together frequently, especially in the summers during vacations on Martha's Vineyard. When my mom was expecting me, her friends hosted a baby shower. One of Mom's gifts was a pink fishing pole for her soon-to-be-born daughter. I loved that fishing rod *so much*! I kept it until I was about nine years old, when I outgrew it for a bigger one. My dad and I also love to swim.

With so much always going on to keep #1000blackgirlbooks running smoothly, my father is trying hard to keep up with our busy schedule. While he is not that good about keeping the monthly calendars, he is great at the day-to-day stuff. He gets me up in the morning and drives me to school most days. Dad also makes breakfast and packs my lunch. On the coldest days, my father makes sure I wear a warm coat. Sometimes he forgets, but he tries. He's the best dad ever.

Dad is always telling me how proud he is of everything I'm trying to achieve. When #1000blackgirlbooks started, Dad was right there to help me get it off the ground. He encouraged me to go for my dream, even though 1,000 books seemed like a really crazy idea at first.

Not only is my dad strong enough to lift boxes of books, and carry crates into our car when Mom and I are transporting materials to schools and community centers, Dad is also strong *inside*.

My dad and me.

Girls Like Me

SMART, FUNNY, INTERESTING, ADVENTUROUS

3

Girls Like Me

SMART, FUNNY, INTERESTING, ADVENTUROUS

That's how I describe the kinds of girls I want to read about. The kinds of girls I know in real life. My friends. Smart, funny, interesting, and adventurous. Brilliant, kind, inquisitive, brave.

Cool, compassionate, and completely amazing.

Girls like me.

Second only to the love and support of my parents is the happiness and strength I can count on from my crew. More than twenty of us make up what we call the SGS: SuperGirls Society. We're a sorority of black girls dedicated to sisterhood and service. Our goal is to use our talents to do good in the world.

Amina, for example—she's the first person to ever call me crazy and I didn't even mind. She loves math more than anything, including cotton candy. Even as a math honors student, I find *that* crazy. But she learned that a lot of the time girls don't go into careers in math or science because they lack math confidence. It's so common across school systems. So she came up with a bunch of games and then hosted a math tournament with a DJ and dancing to make learning it fun instead of the worst. Meanwhile, another friend of mine created a project called Room for Change. With help from Grass-ROOTS and sponsorship from IKEA and Home Depot, she decorated the rooms for homeless teens that stay at the YMCA in Newark, New Jersey. That way, even though they're going through hard times, they'll feel cared for and comfortable. Shea Moisture provided bath and body products, and I provided books for the bedside tables. Together, the three of us also won a Disney Friends for Change $500 grant, which was super exciting. Recognition like that helps make us

> *"My definition of being a boss is setting a personal goal...and achieving it."* – MARLEY DIAS, MADAMENOIRE.COM

with other donations, it helped us a lot.

Working with friends who are committed to social justice and doing good can help make activism fun. The same way Amina wants to make math fun, even though it is also challenging. Activism is hard and fun.

Friends aren't just for causes, obviously. Friends are for hanging out at the mall and making funny

more dedicated to our community activism. While $500 doesn't seem like a lot of money, along

music videos. For blindfolded makeup challenges, impromptu dance shows, and staying up late at sleepovers. They are also for social change. You might think that a society of student activists would be serious 24/7. But we are quite the opposite. We do everything with style!

SUIT AND TIE

I love fashion. Some days I want to be a princess. Some days I want to be a king. Dressing in an

androgynous way, mixing up the masculine and feminine, blurring those boundaries—I'm cool with that. No one should ever be limited by stereotypes of gender, just as no one should ever be limited by stereotypes of race. Lots of fashion-forward people have defied the norms of their time, like Coco Chanel and Prince in the past, and Zendaya and Cara Delevingne—two of my style icons—today. They all exude a confidence I find utterly amazing.

As you probably have noticed by now, I am not some mousy bookworm. On the contrary, I consider myself a fashion-forward person. Yes, you can like school and style simultaneously. The two are not mutually exclusive—one doesn't cancel out the other.

Clothes send a message about who you are. Like it or not, people bring all their own preconceived notions to how you look, and that includes your outfit. They get all judgy before you even open your mouth. So I say it's worth thinking about what statement you want to make.

When I speak at events like EdTek or Black Girls Rock! I prefer to wear suits. Suits say: "I am

Clothes can be curious like that—they end up with histories, even powers, of their own. My grandfather on my dad's side had a North Carolina A&T sweatshirt from when my dad attended college there. And even though

> *"We have different stories, different points of view, different issues in the world. Other people should be able to see that."* — MARLEY DIAS

serious." It's not like I never wear skirts—I wore a swishy black mini on Larry Wilmore's *Nightly Show*—but pants are just more comfortable. I often wear my dad's ties and my mom's earrings. It's a small, almost secret way of having them with me when I'm up there on stage, talking to a roomful of strangers. It makes me feel safe.

I never got to meet my grandfather, just having that sweatshirt now connects the three of us. So it's very special to me. Before she passed, my beautiful great-grandmother on my dad's side gave me her emerald necklace. I don't wear it, I just keep it and hold it in the morning for good luck. It makes me feel connected and I can still keep it safe.

I switch them up with my outfits. The purple ones look like goggles. For Halloween in seventh grade I was the green Powerpuff Girl—Buttercup, the tough tomboy—so I wore my new green frames to go with my costume. My friends Tori and Lizzie played the other two boss superheroes. I also wore green frames when I appeared on *The Ellen DeGeneres Show*, which totally changed my life. Sadly, I broke them over the next summer and had to get the new ones I wear today. My frames have become a piece of me.

My style is intelligent, energetic, silly, and complex. I wear button-up shirts and bright, shiny shoes. But at home after school?

It's leggings, hoodies, and chill.

SPECTACLES

And on the subject of stereotypes . . .

The cliché is that girls who wear glasses are smart. All right, fine, if you insist. But I think glasses are stylish. Like sculptures for your face. I've been wearing them since I was eight. I'm up to nine pairs, and

MY CROWN

Remember how I said before that some days I want to be king? My

> ### "Do _your_ best, don't worry about being _the_ best."
> – MARLEY DIAS

hair is my crown. I've worked thirty-three-plus different styles—I counted. My top five faves are Big Senegalese Twists, Swirled Cornrows, Twist Outs, Straight and Short, and Out and Poufy, aka my Afro. Next up might be waves or a new color—something fun like blue, maybe. I have done *a lot* of things with my hair, but not that. Yet.

Black girl hair has so many meanings. So much history. In

As I mentioned, my mom, Janice, was born and raised in Jamaica, the Caribbean island (which is also a country) where reggae music comes from. When she found out she was pregnant with me, she and my dad talked about how they wanted a child who would think like an adult, laugh like a kid, and have the heart of a lion. That may be why they named me after Jamaican artist and activist Bob Marley (1945-1981), the most popular reggae musician in the world and an advocate for peaceful social change. He has a song, "Iron Lion Zion," which is about his religion, Rastafarianism; he also had a lion tattoo. I even have Bob Marley tunes as the ringtone for the alarm on my phone; it's what I wake up to in the morning. Hear me roar!

Unlike the canine-companioned heroines in some of my imaginary black girl books, I do not have a dog. I don't have a cat either. I *have* had several goldfish, but they all ended up, um, sleeping with the fishes? (They died.) Previous houseplants under my care also have come to an unfortunate end. So I'm trying something new. I now have a whole bunch of succulents to tend. They're supposed to be easier to care for. I've given them all names: Eunice Waymon (better known as Nina Simone, singer), Everett LeRoi Jones (birth name of author-activist Amiri Baraka), Caryn Elaine Johnson (I see you, Whoopi Goldberg, actress), and Erica Abi Wright (oh hey, Erykah Badu, singer). Since the plants are all named after strong and resilient black figures, I figure they just may survive.

the way back, the 1950s and early '60s, it was common for black women to basically burn their scalps with chemical relaxers in order to straighten their kinky hair so that it would conform to white standards of beauty. Ouch. And ugh. And no thank you. That started to change later

in the '60s and '70s, when the civil rights movement embraced natural hair as a symbol of black authenticity. But trends come and go. My nana once made my mom get a Jheri curl, which is a kind of shiny perm—chemicals again!—that was popular in the '80s and '90s. To maintain it, you were supposed to spray your hair with a "curl activator," then apply heavy conditioners, then put it all in a plastic shower cap (!) before you went to bed, to keep your strands slick and smooth. But everyone from pop superstar Michael Jackson—see: the *Thriller* album cover—to legendary rapper Ice Cube had one. My mom *hated* hers. So glad we've moved beyond.

Solange has that song "Don't Touch My Hair." It's about, I think, how lots of girls who wear

why? So weird!) But since I didn't eat sushi, it just wasn't right for me to get one. The toys were too cute, though, so I gave it a try. And yum! Now I eat sushi every week. My favorite types are California, rainbow dragon, and avocado rolls. I do not, however, like the Philly roll, despite the fact that I was born in Philadelphia.

Don't underestimate my chopstick prowess. I am a master. Even as a lefty, which makes lots of ordinary tasks tougher. I can pick up a single grain of rice with chopsticks, dip it in soy sauce, and then write my name on it.

I am *that* good.

When did my obsession with sushi start? I disliked avocado until I was ten, so it couldn't have been till after then. At the mall, I would see these weird, adorable sushi-themed toys. (Because . . .

their hair natural are gawked at and even have their personal space invaded by strangers who touch it without asking permission. Rude! People have tried that with me. But they have failed. Because I am secretly a ninja. Lol, and I have evaded their grasp.

I get that people are intrigued, though. They're uninformed when it comes to black girl hair. They have questions and want to learn more. If my friends ask nicely, sometimes I'll let them touch my hair, especially if it means I'll get a relaxing head massage in return.

That's the bright side of ignorance, lol again.

When I went on *Ellen*, along with the aforementioned, now-long-gone green glasses, I wore my hair in a 'fro—aka Out and

Poufy. It wasn't something I did on a whim; it was a conscious decision. I knew that lots of other young black girls would see me on the show. It was them I was there for, after all, telling our stories, and I wanted them to see themselves reflected in me, just like I want to see us reflected in the books at school. I regard my hair as a gift. The roots of it can be traced back to my ancestral roots in Africa. The way I style it expresses my creativity. The way it can transform into different beautiful shapes from one day to the next symbolizes my grace. All girls deserve to know how empowering that feels, to embrace their natural state and love it for everything it is. Doing my part to help is an honor and a privilege. Black Girl Hair Represent!

My Africa

THE GLOBAL VILLAGE

4

My Africa

THE GLOBAL VILLAGE

Though I didn't know it at the time, my trip to Africa would be important to my campaign and to the way I think about diversity and inclusion. In December 2015, I had the honor of visiting Ghana, a country on the Gulf of Guinea in West Africa. We were there for ten days as part of a health ambassador program with the organization African Health Now. It was a mind-opening experience. Despite the 5,000-mile distance—the whole width of the

Atlantic Ocean—between Accra, the capital city, and my home in New Jersey, some things in Ghana were not so different at all. But others definitely were.

For me as an American-born black person, Africa gave me a new, exciting opportunity to learn. We do not learn much about Africa in school. I suspect that this is on purpose. Though I knew about the enslavement of our people, it was really different to see how and where it happened, and to stand in the places that my ancestors stood and were enslaved. I was inspired by the beauty and the pain. Though everyone we saw was black, each person had their own way of being.

"Africa feels like home."
–MARLEY DIAS

Ghana helped me see myself as part of a much greater whole: of not just my community in America but of the global village. This understanding of and gratitude for my African roots is a gift I'll carry with me forever, as I determine my own destiny in this world.

ARRIVAL

Akwaaba! That's Twi (a Ghanaian language) for "welcome." I can't believe I'm in Africa! Everyone is so friendly. Everyone is black here.

HEALTH FAIR

At the health fair, we helped with dental care, diabetes testing, and blood pressure readings. But we also played with the little kids so that their moms could get their

This is me in Ghana.

checkups in peace! Not everyone has access to health care in Ghana and across the world, so being able to be a part of the experience of helping people become healthy was really important.

DANCE AND GAMES

At the market, the older kids taught me and my friends how to play *ampe*, a game where you jump up, clap your hands, and kick one foot forward—it's almost like a dance, but the winner depends on who puts what foot out. It's fun. We showed the Ghanaian kids how to play slide. By the end, we had all learned something new.

ORPHANAGE

At the Royalhouse Chapel, we served a holiday meal to 766 orphans while a bunch of

Ghanaian celebrities performed for them. I was happy to meet the kids and glad to be a part of an experience that made Christmas an enjoyable moment for them. Afterward, we attended DJ Berla Mundi's Christmas celebration for the kids in the small fishing town of Sakumono.

DANCE COMPETITION

We played outside in the heat and enjoyed the music. Though it was about ninety degrees, the children—like me—loved to dance. They performed a lot of moves that were really hard to do. For the winners of the dance competition, we donated pencils.

DANCE AND UNIVERSAL THEMES

We danced everywhere. We danced at the health fair and we danced at the holiday party. People in Ghana play music and dance at the market and even in the streets. The love of music, and the unity people find in

> *"While the rest of the world has been developing technology, Ghana has been improving the quality of man's humanity to man."* – MAYA ANGELOU

celebration, is the same in Africa as it is in America—or anywhere, I imagine. People love to dance and sing and rejoice.

ELMINA CASTLE

The best and worst day was our visit to Elmina Castle. It was originally built by Portuguese merchants in 1482. It became a major stop on the Atlantic slave trade route: A thousand enslaved Africans were imprisoned there before being shipped abroad to be auctioned off as property. The Door of No Return was a dreaded passageway from the prison to the boats. Enslaved Africans were sent either to Brazil, the Caribbean, or the United States. Upsetting to see, but it's so important to know my history. I was really glad I went. I learned so much but cried while I was there, and I sometimes cry thinking about how horribly our ancestors were treated.

Elmina Castle.

A colorful Ghanaian market.

W. E. B. DuBOIS CENTRE

The great black academic and activist W. E. B. DuBois spent the last years of his life in Ghana. What did I do at the center dedicated to his legacy? Read in the library, of course! They had to kick us out because I got so caught up in reading.

GHANAIAN PEOPLE AND FASHION

I loved seeing the way people dressed in Ghana; it was so beautiful. I loved the mixture of vibrant

printed fabrics and took home several head wraps. The clothing there inspired my outfit at Black Girls Rock! I added some of the patterns to my suit to give it its own unique style.

CUISINE IN GHANA

For the first time, I tried jollof rice, which gave me life. And the steamed rice balls are one of my favorite foods ever.

GHANA IN GENERAL

Every single place you went there were black people. Black people were on billboards and on every corner. There is diversity where I live, but outside of school and SuperGirls Society you don't see a

GHANA IN GENERAL

Ghana helped boost my identity by connecting me to the continent. I really enjoyed seeing that children there like children in the United States participate in similar things. Ghana showed me diversity among black people, and it also showed me the universal nature of being a young person.

lot of black people. In Ghana it's just, like, OK, I'm black, you're black, everybody's black. It felt really nice and different.

Oh So Social

I *COULD* GOOGLE MYSELF, BUT…

5

Oh So Social

I *COULD* GOOGLE MYSELF, BUT ...

Social media and *social* activism are about community. While activism is largely "boots on the ground," taking place in your city or town, clicktivism lives online—out there in the ether, on the interwebs.

For something so abstract, its power is real and intense.

Personally, I love my phone and the way it can connect me to readers in every corner of the globe. A huge part of the success of #1000blackgirlbooks is thanks to social media. But . . . let's just say that me and the web, we got off to a bumpy start.

It's always been very important to me and my mom and dad to use social media for good, and to be safe while doing it. Parents are the ones who give their kids permission to be on social media. The companies that create social media platforms have very strict rules about how old a person has to be to get a social media account. My hashtag was used by my parents before I was allowed to. That's because there's even something called the Children's Online Privacy Protection Act (aka, COPPA) that prevents companies from collecting

> ## *"Social media is a great tool for creating social change."* –MARLEY DIAS

certain information from kids under age thirteen. To set up any social media account, you have to be thirteen or older to have an account. And if you're under thirteen, you still can't get an account with your parents' consent.

I'd come up with the hashtag over pancakes, as you'll recall. The next obvious step was to send my brave little hashtag out into the world. In the very beginning of the campaign, I'd pose for photos with black girl books, holding them up to show the cover and acting as if I were reading them. (I had read them all already, of course! I wasn't just posing for the pictures.) Then my mom posted them to Facebook, Instagram, and Twitter—this was

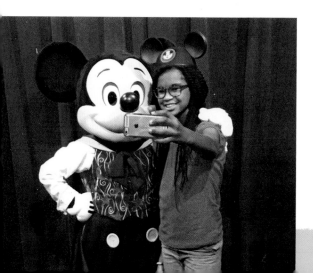

a few years ago now; I was a lot younger, and I didn't have a social media account then.

Because I launched my campaign when I was eleven years old, my parents helped me create my social media presence, and they closely monitored all the activity surrounding my social media. Even though I'm a teenager now, they still supervise everything I do on social media.

When I was planning my campaign, my parents' input helped me go viral in the safest and most responsible way. And now that #1000blackgirlbooks is up and running, that's still the case. Mom and Dad are by my social media side at every moment. When Mom or Dad give me the thumbs-up, I know they are OK with what I've posted.

I'm glad my parents have

Mom, Dad, and me at The Ellen DeGeneres Show.

82

> ## "Social media is a tool . . . use it for good." —MARLEY DIAS

always been so cautious, because I don't know how I would have dealt with the incident that happened soon after my campaign got started. My mom only told me about it after. Some deplorable troll saw one of my photos on Facebook and replied by threatening me, commenting that if I "wanted to see black people" I should "look in the prisons. Or read the obituaries."

I know.

I mean . . .

Just no.

Ninety-nine percent of the time, I strive not to focus on the negative. Ninety-nine percent of the time, I believe the best plan of action is to keep pushing forward on the positive: "When they go low, we go high," to quote the supreme Michelle Obama. But let me just take a breath here, for one brief moment, and get real. For the record, just this once, let me say:

Hard things come and go, but it seems like racism always stays.

There, I said it.

And I'm doing all I can to change it.

Peace and love.

Moving on . . .

Mom, me, and Michelle Obama.

The magic of social media, though, is that for this one crazy troll, there were thousands of complete strangers who had my back. Not only did they shut down the troll for those ugly comments, they spread my hashtag too. Twitter was a big part of it—400,000 tweets! Thank you, Black Twitter! Respect! But it wasn't only Black Twitter: It was anyone who'd ever felt unheard or ignored. I was the messenger, but it was the message, about the need for diversity and inclusion, that made it feel so real to everyone.

Ironically, you could almost claim that I should thank the troll for stirring up such a perfect storm. But nope. Not gonna.

Suddenly, #1000blackgirlbooks was being retweeted, my videos and links shared on Facebook . . . the whole thing just went viral. Up till that point I had been wondering (worrying) how, exactly, I was going to reach my goal of 1,000. Social media solved that for me. The donations began pouring in. TV shows started having me on as a guest. Ellen DeGeneres gave me a check for $10,000 (!!!). At last count, we've received some 10,000 books. By the time you're reading this, it will be more.

So yes, social media can be used for good, not just makeup tutorials, cat and slime videos, and angry tweets. Though who doesn't love a cute cat video?

MY FAVORITE PAGES

These sites are bookmarked on my browser and loaded onto my phone.

YouTube: Oh, hello, did I mention I love cat videos?

Google Classroom: I get a lot of my language arts assignments here. It's homeschooling on a computer—I can talk with the other kids in my class even if I'm not there.

Spotify: I listen when I'm in the shower and working on projects.

(No, not at the same time: The ink would run!) Because I don't have premium, I end up hearing a lot of gratuitous profanity. Way to go, parents.

NETFLIX: For binge-watching *Phineas and Ferb* and weird documentaries, like the one about Elmo. (Yes, that Elmo. There is no other.)

ELLE.com: I had the amazing opportunity to guest-edit *Elle*'s online magazine, and the experience only made me more determined to be a magazine editor one day. I read the site daily for my Capricorn horoscope and to keep up with Fashion Week.

PowerSchool: To track my grades. Sometimes I check them multiple times in a week. Hashtag obsessed!

BuzzFeed: I take every quiz. Every. Single. One.

Me with Tina Tchen, Valerie Jarrett, Melissa Harris-Perry.

CLICKTIVISM 101

How to use online platforms to further your cause . . .

1 CLAP BACK • My encounter with the troll perfectly illustrates the impact of the clap back. When an online group such as Black Twitter rallies to your defense, it can quickly flip the script of a situation: The victim of online harassment (e.g., me) is validated, and the troll is shouted back into its cave—I visualize the person as being in dirty pj's in front of an old TV, surrounded by greasy fast-food wrappers. But even without the community support, remember: Everything on the internet is optional. I know it can seem beyond real when you're caught up in the thick of a social media war, but there's a simple, super-effective strategy to remove yourself from drama: Just unfollow the offender. Unsubscribe from their page. Block 'em! I do that on Instagram, Twitter, and YouTube all the time. It will give you peace of mind, and it has the added bonus of driving trolls crazy, since so much of the noise online is from people who want to call attention to themselves, to rack up "likes" and followers. Your mental energy is precious:

Don't waste it on them. Just say so long, farewell, sayonara, good-bye! It's important to note, though, that a lone troll who sends out a few terrible messages is one thing. But sometimes a single misunderstood tweet coming from your end could cause negative attention for you—and the grown-ups who are helping you—outside of the social media bubble in the *real* world. In some situations, kids have sent out their 140-character opinions without thinking, and people form the wrong impression about them or their family members. Tweeting hastily is like blurting out something you didn't mean to say, then regretting it later. So please—think before you tweet or post! If you have any doubts about a tweet, show it to your parents before sending it off, which is definitely advisable if you'd like to . . .

2 THROW RIGHTEOUS SHADE • The clap back and the unfollow aren't just effective tactics for shutting down personal attacks from random trolls: They work wonders on politicians, other prominent figures, and organizations too. Like in the book *Holes* by Louis Sachar, the internet today is an open space to basically shame wrongdoers in public. Whenever someone doesn't do what they are supposed to, they get in trouble and are made fun of by everyone. If you want to pressure a company that engages in bad practices— whether it's gender discrimination

SENSITIVE CONVERSATIONS

"We need to talk": Those four little words can stop anyone cold in their high-tops; rarely does anything good follow them. No one ever says, "We need to talk about how you need to eat more ice cream" or "We need to talk about why your grades are too good." But to call attention to prejudice, sometimes you've got to suck it up and have an awkward and occasionally hard conversation. For suggestions on how to discuss racism, sexism, microaggressions, and other touchy subjects with friends or family members, check out "Speak Up: Responding to Everyday Bigotry," a handy online guide from the Southern Poverty Law Center: tolerance.org/lesson/discovering-my-identity

or excess carbon emissions or some other nonsense—call them out on Twitter and Facebook. Tag them directly and add a hashtag that sums up your frustration, like #noplasticbags or #recyclenow. Others who agree with you will pile on, retweeting and reposting. Companies hate that, because the negative publicity damages their brand and their profits. The louder the clap back gets, the faster they'll scramble to make it stop, even if it means changing their policies. You might also want to check out such groups as Sleeping Giants, which targets businesses that advertise on sites that publish hateful content. Shining the spotlight on them can force them to withdraw their ads, which are a primary source of income for the websites.

3 KEEP COOL • One thing about social media: Everything (and I mean everything) you say is permanent.

Once it's out there, it's out there. No take-backs. Even if you delete something, it's there forever. So you have to think carefully about what you say, how you say it, why you say it, and who you're saying it to. Like I said, you should have a parent or adult helping you here, but still, take time to think it through. Throwing shade may feel righteous, but sometimes a simple conversation—a meeting, a phone call—might accomplish more (and . . . um . . . that's hard to do after you've called folks out on Twitter). Remember what your goals are, and don't scare away potential allies before you've given them a chance. Getting creative and keeping true to your voice is also important, but don't forget that you're speaking to hundreds, potentially thousands, of people. Double-check your tweets and posts before clicking the button—is it possible that people will miss your point? Your pics, status updates, and tweets won't

Staying cool on social media is important.

always be perfect, but social media won't forgive you for big mistakes. It can be a pain to always have to be so careful, but it will save you in the end. People have lost their jobs, received threats, and faced other horrible consequences for posting things they thought were funny (at the time), only to realize their mistake later. Good rule of thumb: Be proud of what you post!

4 **STAY OUT OF THE COMMENTS** • From the time I was little, my parents were strict about me crossing the street carefully, and staying away from places where there's a lot of crazy traffic. The same is true of social media. It moves super-fast, and there's a lot of "traffic." It's tempting to respond quickly to comments (I admit to having some fast thumbs), but I've learned to think before writing back on a message (like taking the time to look both ways before crossing the street). To make it easy, I stay out of arguments by not reading comments very often. Since I can't comment back to everyone, I keep it simple. When I do comment, it's often on Instagram, and I usually only read the first one or two messages. When I comment, Mom or Dad reads what I'm saying first, then OKs it before my thumbs go to work and press send. And—my parents have laid down the law. They shadow my account. I had to agree to this, or kiss social media good-bye. It's all fine with me. (I still cross the street with one of my parents if they're nearby.) Once I post on Instagram or Twitter, I tend to walk away for a week or so. I tweet a lot when I'm at an event. I try to stay engaged for a day or two, but then I stay off it. I did a school debate and report on kids who are on social media a lot. There are social and emotional downsides to social media, if you don't manage or control yourself. I think everyone gets trolled. The best thing to do is to ignore. Real people matter more. Cyber people are not real. They don't know me, so I try not to make them matter too much.

5 GET PERSONAL • I could throw statistics around all day about the low percentage of books featuring black characters on school curricula or in library collections and blah blah blah. I could, but that

BLACKISH GIRL MAGIC

I love how Marsai Martin steals every scene as the sassy and brilliant Diane Johnson on *Blackish*: She brought that same boss attitude when she joined me on my literacy tour. We decided to join our superpowers to show youth that reading can be fun.

We launched a reading party at the Department of Education in Washington, DC, with two hundred black girls, in collaboration with a White House Initiative on Educational Excellence for African Americans. In the future, we'll travel to other cities where we want to get adults and children excited about black girls' stories, and about reading.

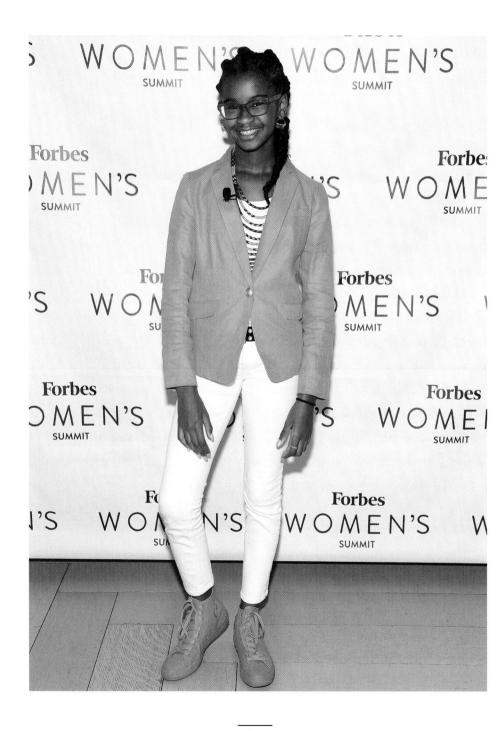

would probably put you (and definitely me) to sleep. To get across your message, it always helps to make it personal instead. That's what sticks in people's minds—not dry facts and data. If you're comfortable doing so and your parents say it's OK, post about your own experience in your own words. Maybe you've faced discrimination or racism yourself. Maybe you have a family member who's suffering from the disease you want to raise money to cure. Maybe neglectful behavior by businesses and politicians has resulted in something terrible, like water poisoned with lead or parks littered with trash. How has it impacted you? How does it make you feel? What do you want your community to do about it? By using social media to show and tell what matters to you, you are promoting your values.

6 GET CREATIVE • If you love to write, draw, dance, or sing, then do that. Express your experience in the way that feels most authentic to who you are, and then put it out there for the world to see. If you're frustrated that the voices of your kind (however you self-identify) aren't being represented in popular culture or the political climate, one way to combat that is to use your own! It's so obvious it's easy to overlook: If you want to be heard, make some noise! Your voice, your opinion, your experience, your life *matters*—just as much as anyone else's.

7 **#SMALLACTS** • I don't know who started this—I googled but couldn't find it—and I'm too crazed now writing this book to research more. So props to whoever did it first. Oh, that's another magic thing about social media: These movements sort of spring up; it's hard to pinpoint exactly how or why. It's like they suddenly arise to fill a need. Anyway, this hashtag is exactly what it sounds like: You do #smallacts—either to protest injustice or promote positive things—and then tag it and share it on Twitter to inspire other people. The point is that even the smallest deed can make a big difference; that just one person (you!) can change the dynamic. One of my favorite—and easiest—#smallacts is just to add emojis instead of punctuation marks in my post. Using emojis makes my post more vibrant, and it shares how I'm feeling. It gives people a sense of joy. And chances are it cheers up whoever is reading my post. Some people like to use

RUNNING THIS TOWN

When I met Rihanna at the Black Girls Rock! awards show, she told me that it was important to have black girls out there trying to make the world better.

Me speaking at the New York Women's Foundation.

Post-its. P.S.: In November 2016, after the presidential election, many people in the city of New York did this spontaneously—see page 119.

Social media offers an amazing space for you to broadcast your own truth and connect with others who support your position. For those who are like me and are young, remember you need to talk to a caring and motivated adult so they can help you be safe while using social media.

To have a real impact on your community, though, you also have to come out from behind the glow of your computer screen and into the clear light of day. Tweeting and posting on Instagram can be incredible ways to spread the word, but they can also be a bit passive. And I think it's about time we got *active*.

Be the Change You Want to See in the World

GET WOKE!

6

Be the Change You Want to See in the World

GET WOKE!

Back in the beginning of the book, when I introduced the principles I've learned from being a part of GrassROOTS, I talked about the importance of Truth, Order, Reciprocity, and Balance. Here's another mantra that I try to live by: "Be the change you want to see in the world." Meaning, identify the issues in your community you think are unfair, and then take action to change them. Here's where this book's subtitle comes in—And So Can *You*! Because you *can* get it done.

I know I make it sound so simple, right? Well, it sort of is, but it's not *easy*. It takes hard work for sure, and it could take a long time. But it's not too complicated either, if that makes sense. It's just a question of patience and passion, and of applying the tactics I describe below.

Lots of times people have big ideas about changing the world, but what world? It's wherever you are, right now. City, suburb, countryside. North, south, east, west. Doesn't matter. Ultimately, all these issues matter to us—whether it's racial inequality,

illiteracy, or climate change—all these things are personal. They don't only impact the planet at large—they impact us. You and me. If *we* care about them, we can use our passion to make other people care about them too. To throw one more motto into the mix, there's a reason activists often say, "Think global, act local." I try to change the world by collecting and donating books with the help of many hands working together. This is called (get ready, big word) a *coalition*, which means "combined action." So are you and your friends ready to rise and shine, and to join me? What I'm really asking you is . . .

ARE YOU WOKE?

You're reading this book, so you must be. Yay you! Way to become informed about, and understanding of, the different types of people and problems that surround you.

Sad-but-not-exactly-shocking, though, lots of folk are not woke. Not yet, at least. Don't hate on 'em. It's not always their fault. They usually don't mean to be blind to the injustices other people—often minority or marginalized people—have to deal with on the daily. Most unwoke (or those who are asleep) honestly don't know any better, either because they've never identified with or been impacted by overt injustice or—possibly more disturbing—they have, and they don't even realize it. Part of your challenge as an activist is to enlighten those who, for whatever reason, are still asleep.

Remember, now: The unwoke are like the undead. That's right, I said it: zombies. They're functional but slow. Stumbling through life. Unlike the undead, the unwoke *won't* want to eat your brain. But if only they did! Then they could digest all your knowledge. *Mmmm,* sweet, tasty knowledge . . .

Instead, you'll have to educate them the old-fashioned way: through calm, logical, convincing conversations. Probably several long conversations. Over a period of time. Awakening the unwoke is a process. But you can do it! Recognizing what level someone is at in her or his personal

> *"The unwoke are like the undead. That's right, I said it: zombies. They're functional but slow."*
>
> —MARLEY DIAS

evolution will help you gauge how to proceed.

LEVEL 1: AWARENESS:

Good news: There is a spark here—awareness that a problem exists. But the person doesn't know the details and is not making an effort to learn them. Typical response (mumbled): "Yeah, I think I maybe heard something about that." (Changes subject.) "Wanna get some sushi?"

LEVEL 2: CONSCIOUSNESS:

OK, progress has been made. Conscious people understand the meaning of a situation, can break it down into cause and effects, and can even admit that something should be done. They're just not willing to do it themselves, or don't know how. Typical response (said while pulling a shruggie like: ¯_(ツ)_/¯): "But what can you do?"

LEVEL 3: WOKENESS:

Ahhh . . . enlightenment. The person is aware of the problem, conscious of its complexity, and ready to act. That is, she or he is ready to become an *activist* for change. Typical response (announced between bites on a protein bar): "Not on my watch!"

WOKENESS (OR NOT) AS REPRESENTED BY CARTOON PRINCESSES

AWARE: CINDERELLA

Cooking, cleaning, and sewing for her abusive stepmother and sisters? Cinderella was definitely oppressed because of her gender and her class (being the poor step-daughter). Too bad her only way out of one bad situation was to conform to another stereotype by having a prince rescue her based on her dainty foot size. Fitting into a glass slipper is *not* the same thing as shattering the glass ceiling!

CONSCIOUS: JASMINE

She could see the financial divide between those who lived in the palace and those who didn't. She knew that the world around her was rigged to favor the 1 per-cent—rich people and royalty. But Jasmine did nothing about it—it never even occurred to her, probably—till she fell in love with a poor "bad boy," Aladdin, who "opened her eyes" (like they sing in that song when they're taking the carpet ride). Only then does she want her father, the sultan, to change the rules. Better late than never, Jasmine!

WOKE: MULAN AND BELLE

Now we're getting somewhere. Mulan is a feminist. She fights against the patriarchy (that's a society governed by men) by impersonating a boy in order to join the army, since she wasn't allowed to as a girl (argh! the patriarchy!). She does this to keep her own sick and elderly father from getting drafted, which is still kinda protecting the patriarchy, but nevertheless: It's progress. By challenging sexism in the military, Mulan made a difference.

For her part, Belle took a stance against lookism: She showed the angry townspeople that the Beast should not be discriminated against based on his appearance. She showed that people should be judged on the content of their character, not the shagginess of their fur. And by doing so, she helped the Beast see his own beauty within. Plus, Belle is a major book geek and loves a library, so she's my type of girl.

ASLEEP: SNOW WHITE AND SLEEPING BEAUTY

Could it be any more obvious? These two are a couple of snoozers, just dozing along with the status quo. One of them even has *Sleeping* in her name! I mean . . . really!!

CHARITY ≠ ACTIVISM

Charity is not activism. Don't misunderstand—I think charity is awesome. I participate in a lot of charitable events and support charitable organizations when-, where-, and however I can. But there's a difference between charity and activism. And it's a difference you should know as you're deciding which way you want to move forward to make a change in the world.

You can drag old coats out from the back of your closet and donate them to a clothing drive, or even if you give your loose change to a homeless person on the street, you are practicing charity. It's a one-way thing: You give something to someone in need, you hope it helps them, and you go on with your day.

Activism is *reciprocal*: There's a give-and-take. It's about teaching, but it's also about learning. It involves actions that create direct, meaningful impact and change—change that will benefit not just other people, but also you! With the #1000blackgirl-books campaign, yes, I donate

lots and lots of books to communities that need them, which is charitable of me and all the amazing people involved in the campaign. But I don't just do it out of the goodness of my heart: I also want to *see* black girl books on more school mandatory reading lists, including books I write. I want to change the way we imagine and think about black girls. These are the primary goals behind my appearances on TV and at other events. That's me "being the change." I've had some success too, btw. Because of #1000blackgirlbooks, Rita Williams-Garcia's *One Crazy Summer* was added to the curriculum of my old elementary school in New Jersey. Now hundreds of children can re-image black girls!

The Difference: An activist wouldn't just donate. She would text all her friends (you always need your community with you) and get them to donate with her. Instead of just dropping off bags of groceries, she would stay to help serve meals, clear tables, and wash dishes. She would talk with the people she's feeding and listen to their stories. *An activist is engaged.*

Talking and listening: This may sound like a small act. *But it's not.* It can be downright revolutionary. How else will we ever understand other people's problems, challenges, and points of view if we don't hear them? Hear their truth. In their own words.

That's the power of stories, after all.

So not only would an activist help out at the soup kitchen, she might also reach out to her local government offices to find out what else she and her friends could do toward ending the problem. A solution could involve anything from promoting better access to healthy food to helping build affordable housing—through a group like Habitat for Humanity, for example. An activist is always looking to make lasting changes. Think sustainability.

See the difference? Charity is like the pebble you drop in still water. Activism is the ripples upon ripples of waves that radiate out from it, the circles growing wider and wider and reaching farther and farther to touch as many people as possible.

IMAGINE, SEE, BELIEVE, ACHIEVE

You're woke. You got the fire. You got a cause that's close to your heart. But you're too young to vote. Too young to run for office. Now what?

Imagine the way you want things to be. Stephen Covey, who wrote *The 7 Habits of Highly Effective People,* says: "Begin with the end in mind." Imagine how things would look if you solved the problem. It's easier to get help when you can share your vision with others.

Here's how:

START SMALL.

Engaging in small but meaningful acts like those described later in this chapter is a good way to begin. You'll be able to see the impact of your activism and then adjust and expand your approach as you continue.

PACE YOURSELF.

And have fun. If you feel more anxious than excited about your cause, or if the effort you're putting into it is exhausting instead of energizing you, reevaluate. Have you bitten off more than you can chew? Do you maybe not feel as strongly about the issue as you first thought? That's perfectly OK. You can always stop and start anew.

SHARE YOUR GOAL.

Tell the people closest to you—your family, your friends, the teachers you trust—and *ask* for their help so that you don't end up overwhelmed and alone. Social activism is supposed to be just that: social! And everyone needs a team. Even if all they can offer is moral support and sushi, accept it! Surround yourself with as many cheerleaders as you can get, because keeping your confidence up is half the battle. And eat as many

ONE CRAZY SUMMER, by Rita Williams-Garcia, tells the story of Delphine, Vonetta, and Fern, three sisters from Brooklyn, New York, who spend the summer of 1968 in Oakland, California, with their estranged mom, Cecile. Their mom is a poet who's involved with the Black Panthers, an activist party that sometimes used radical tactics to promote the rights of minorities.

When Cecile gets arrested, the girls . . . well, no spoilers! Read it and find out for yourself. The book is so good: It was a National Book Award finalist, a Newbery Honor recipient, and won the Scott O'Dell Award for Historical Fiction. You end up learning about the civil rights movement of the late 1960s without even realizing it.

of your favorite foods as you can, because being happy and fed is necessary for any revolution.

ASK QUESTIONS.

Learn as much as you can about your cause: Ask how the problem began in the first place, why it's still happening now, and what the different sides of the debate believe. Become the expert and spread the facts. Check out the Activist's Toolbox on page 126 for some ideas on how to stay informed.

REMEMBER AND RECHECK YOUR GOALS.

What are you trying to accomplish? If your goal is to call attention to an issue, getting tons of good publicity may do the trick. If you want to actually put a stop to harmful behavior, then positive, dramatic actions could be the most effective way to apply pressure to the wrongdoers. But if your aim is to raise money, you probably need to make nice with anyone who has a wallet. Tailor your tactics to your target result. In other words . . .

CHOOSE A PROTEST STYLE.

There are many ways to approach a problem: One isn't necessarily better than another, and a combo—a bento box or sushi platter, if you prefer—of tactics is often a recipe for success. So it's more a question of what you feel most comfortable doing and what (drumroll, please) GETS IT DONE (thank you, thank you, high fives all around). Not sure what your strategy should be? No worries. That's what I'm here for. From least demanding to most involved, I've put together a convenient activist's primer for you. You're welcome!

THIS IS HOW WE ACTIVATE: 14 DIFFERENT WAYS TO MAKE A DIFFERENCE

Now it's time to put our passion into boots-on-the-ground action. With the help of my parents, I've participated in most of these kinds of events. Others I've learned about while doing research for this book. As a kid, I've relied a lot on adults for guidance and have let them show me the best ways to be an activist, and stay safe while doing it. A word of advice: If you're a kid like me, I recommend doing the same thing. Get adults to help you. After all, they're bigger, louder, and can get other adults to be on your team. (Did I mention that parents like to brag about the positive things their kids are doing? By letting them help you, you're also giving them the "my-kid-is-the-greatest" bragging rights they love so much!)

Me, feminist trailblazer Gloria Steinem, and Mom.

1 DONATE • Food or clothes or school supplies. Old computers or cell phones. Or books! (I'm working so that black girls are represented, but maybe you have a different literary niche.) If there's a need, give whatever you can to fill it. If there's a well-established nonprofit organization that supports your cause, you can invite your caregivers to check it out first, then ask them if you can use their credit card to set up a small recurring contribution—$5 a month or more—which you can pay back out of your allowance or the money you earn through babysitting or other jobs.

2 VOLUNTEER • Even if you cleaned out your pantry, your closets, and the attic, you've still got something more to give: your time. Contact a local group that reflects your values and offer them your services. Libraries almost always need after-school tutors. Senior centers and nursing home residents appreciate visitors who will play anything from Scrabble to the piano with them. Or how about dog walking? Think of all the happily wagging tails of shelter pups. Some places may have age restrictions on volunteering, so best to find out first.

3 ORGANIZE A DRIVE • As I touched upon before, when I was explaining the difference between charity and activism—it's charitable for you to donate your own stuff. It's a bit more activist to get your friends to donate too. The next level would be to host a full-on drive through your school or your church, synagogue, or mosque, or other community organization. It makes it more fun if you set a clear, ambitious, but doable target, like I did with 1,000 books.

Families who live in shelters, for example, often urgently need such basics as diapers and socks. So take a cue from Captain Underpants, divide your grade into teams—Socks vs. Pampers—and whoever reaches the goal number first wins a pizza party. Tra-la-la!

4 CIRCULATE A PETITION

In the next chapter, I'll tell you how to actually pick up the phone and call the politicians elected to represent you. Like, speak with your voice. Out loud. Without emojis. Or abbreviations. (Though talking on the phone is not something people my age like to do as much as our parents and grandparents did, it ends up that old-fashioned phone calls have the most impact on senators and congresspersons because so many of them are the same age as our grandparents!) Petitions may

As a student, Barack Obama was editor of the Harvard Law Review.

You know who got his start as a community organizer? This guy! Former president Barack Obama called his three years as a grassroots organizer "the best education I ever had, better than anything I got at Harvard Law School."

Hmmm. If it's good enough for the first black president of the United States, maybe you should give community activism a try too!

not be as influential as individual phone calls—and emails and letters, all of which are logged and recorded separately by your elected representatives' offices. But there's power in numbers. Through online research, you will almost certainly find a pre-existing petition that supports your cause—don't stress, it's not like you have to start one from scratch! If you can get as many people as possible in your circle to electronically sign, it all adds up. And petitions are especially useful when you're trying to reach politicians who *don't* represent your district or state but who may have a powerful impact on the debate. If they receive a petition with literally millions of signatures from all across the country, it's hard for them to ignore that consensus. Tip: If you get 100,000 signatures, the White House has to respond. It used to be just 25,000. ☹

5 ATTEND TOWN COUNCIL OR COMMUNITY BOARD MEETINGS • Will it be boring? Parts of it, probably. But while national politics can seem remote, with change difficult to achieve, local politics are much easier to affect. I think it may even be more important to work right in your neighborhood or town. The smaller scale means there's a much bigger chance for your opinion to be heard, especially during the portion of meetings when public questions or comments are allowed. Raise your hand, stand up, state your piece: It will be entered into the public record, and you can ask—your mayor or the superintendent of your school district, for example—about what actions will be taken to address your concerns and how you can follow up on them. Once these local officials hear your concerns, they are in the position to amplify them.

6 CHECK CALENDARS • Have you noticed how there's a day for everything? And I mean *everything*. December 5, for example, is International Ninja Day. I am not kidding. (It's also International Volunteer Day.) Earth Day is April 22. International Literacy Day: September 8. World Turtle Day: May 23. World Diabetes Day: November 14. Basically, google either your issue, to find out the day it's recognized, or google the month to see what holidays might be

coming up. Depending on how they fit into your plans, you can bring more attention to your cause if you celebrate—or protest, as the case may be—on the same day as the rest of the world.

Here I am, speaking up!

7 BE AN UPSTANDER •

A *by*stander is someone who stands *by* and watches while something—something bad—happens. An *up*stander is someone who steps up and steps in to help. If you see bullying or harassment happening—if someone is being singled out for their race or religion, gender, or appearance—be brave and speak up. Don't confront the bully directly—that could be dangerous. But help escort the person who is being hurt away from the situation and to a safe place. Talk to them to make sure they're OK. And call for help if necessary. Also, although I can't 100 percent guarantee this,

I'd bet that once you speak up, you'll inspire other bystanders to become upstanders too.

8 COLOR COORDINATE •

I personally love this method of protest so hard because it combines two of my favorite things: activism and fashion. Specific items of clothing in symbolic colors can be powerful symbols and send strong messages. It's why millions of women wore pink hats to marches on January 21, 2017, to protest sexism. And it's why the Black Lives Matter movement has adopted the black hoodie to protest racial profiling. This is in part

to remember Trayvon Martin, the unarmed seventeen-year-old who was shot to death in 2012 by a man in his Florida neighborhood who claimed the boy was an intruder just because he was wearing a similar sweatshirt. In the early 1900s, the suffragettes wore white while marching for women's right to vote. If you can connect a particular color to your personal cause, consider it a way to make a statement by showing, and without saying a word.

Ida B. Wells-Barnett, one of my civil rights sheroes.

9 OH, BOY(COTT) • Boycotting is about not putting your money where your mouth is. It's about not supporting businesses that don't represent your values. If you're against makeup being tested on animals, don't buy cosmetic brands that do. If you're worried about child labor, research retailers of cheap "fast fashion" to find out all you can about their practices and factories before you spend money at their shops. Both brand loyalty and repeat business are super important to companies. By withholding yours—and spreading the word on social media about your reasons why, as described in Chapter 5—you *will* make a difference.

You can also boycott by "unfollowing" or "unliking" and "unsubscribing" to organizations and people who endorse ideas that you object to or who support companies and ideas that are in direct opposition to the things you value.

10 TAKE A SEAT •

Sit-ins are a passive, peaceful form of protest. Basically, you "occupy" a space and refuse to move until your demands are met. The most famous sit-ins in American history are those that took place during the civil rights movement, such as the one in 1960 when four black college students sat at the lunch counter of a Woolworth's in Greensboro, North Carolina. Because they were sitting in the Whites Only section of a segregated restaurant, they were refused service. But they remained seated. This one nonviolent act of protest blossomed, and soon African Americans, students, church groups, and others sympathetic to the cause began protesting segregated businesses. Both the bad publicity and the loss of income pressured the companies

to change their policies. All of these actions led the government to pass the Civil Rights Act of 1964, finally outlawing racial segregation. Today, the Greensboro lunch counter and stools that the four college-age boys occupied is part of the collection of the Smithsonian's National Museum of American History. More recently, during the Great Recession, the group Occupy Wall Street set up camp in Zuccotti Park, near the Financial District in Lower Manhattan, to protest the growing gap between the rich and the poor. In Standing Rock, North Dakota, protestors occupied a historic Native American reservation where an oil pipeline was (and still is) scheduled to be built. In both Zuccotti Park and Standing Rock, occupiers were eventually cleared out, so we do not know yet what impact their protests will have. But often protests like those I just talked about make a difference by educating people and calling attention to an important issue, even if the protestors don't immediately succeed in putting a stop to a specific problem.

11 STAGE A PERFORMANCE

These are still nonviolent, but a bit more open and expressive. They definitely make their position known, even if they annoy and upset some people in the process—and that's the whole point. Sometimes performance protests serve as a kind of release of pent-up frustrations and emotions. For example, after the presidential election in November 2016, many New Yorkers were so depressed and freaked out that they started leaving random sticky notes on the walls of the Union Square subway station. Some notes were angry; others were sad. Some expressed support for Muslims, Mexicans, and other minority communities that the president-elect had criticized. The sticky notes were in a rainbow of neon colors, and the whole wall turned into this living piece of art that was actually kind of beautiful. So much so that the New-York Historical Society decided to preserve as much of it as possible. The "therapy wall" made New Yorkers feel more connected to one another during a very stressful time. It also showed their combined creativity, and it inspired lots of people and gave them hope. This is a major achievement.

Other types of performance protests can be more specific though. People for the Ethical Treatment of Animals (PETA)

has been known to splash buckets of red paint on fur coats—and the women wearing them. Just a few years ago, "glitter bombing" had a moment, when LGBTQA+ activists doused politicians who opposed gay marriage with handfuls of, yes, glitter. Not harmful, but shocking. Happily, in June 2015, the Supreme Court ruled that same-sex marriage was legal in all fifty states.

12 TAKING IT TO THE STREETS • To know where we're marching into the future, it's important to look at the past. This is like the Sankofa bird. In our affirmation from SuperCamp, we say, "We look to our past so we can be our best today and every day." Black people have been at the forefront of some of the most impressive and impactful marches in America's history. We have not done this alone. We have always worked in collaboration and cooperation with people of all races and ethnicities.

There have been lots of protest marches that serve as great examples for how we can all come together to make a change in the world.

The Selma to Montgomery marches are among the most meaningful to me because so many young people participated. These were several protests that happened in 1965. People walked

along a 54-mile highway from Selma, Alabama, to the state capital of Montgomery.

Like all great marches, these were very well organized. Black citizens were protesting for their right to vote. They were also marching to end segregation (black and white people had to be separate in public places like movie theaters, restaurants, and yes, even libraries!).

On "Bloody Sunday," March 7, 1965, 600 protesters left Selma and started walking along US Route 80. But they didn't get very far. At the Edmund Pettus Bridge, which was only six blocks away, they were attacked with billy clubs and tear gas, and then forced back into Selma by the police. Two days later, on March 9, Dr. Martin Luther King Jr. led another march to the bridge.

Those were some of the bravest and most determined people! Their example continues to inspire

That's me, completely starstruck, with director Ava DuVernay. I had an hour-long convo with her about her movie *Selma*, which tells the story of Dr. Martin Luther King's epic 1965 march from Selma to Montgomery, Alabama, for the cause of black voting rights. I loved the movie, and cried through the whole thing. And I told her so! We have a common interest in that we both want to make sure that our stories—of black girls and women—are told. Meeting her in person—in swelteringly hot New Orleans—was super, super cool.

Ava is also the mastermind behind the film version of one of my favorite books that she adapted into a major motion picture, *A Wrinkle in Time* by Madeleine L'Engle.

In Ava's film version of the story, she's made the main character, Meg Murry, a biracial girl. How cool is that?

me and so many others. Lots of good things came out of the Selma marches. They made people see that, yes, racial injustice was real. The Selma marches also contributed to the Voting Rights Act of 1965 being passed and other civil rights injustices being changed.

I was honored to meet with director Ava DuVernay, who documented Dr. King's march from Selma to Montgomery in her movie *Selma*. As the film pointed out, even though the people who took part in the Selma marches were brave and committed, it took a while before anything changed. Progress was slow, but it did happen. But like I said before, we are not done. We have to keep working every day to make the world a better place and to end inequality.

On January 21, 2017, people from all over the United States came to Washington, DC, and many more marched across the nation and the world to fight for women's rights. There were "sister

marches" in more than 300 cities in the United States alone. It was the single largest moment of protest in America ever. An estimated three million people took part, according to the statistics website FiveThirtyEight. Millions of women and girls, lots of them wearing those pink hats, marched for gender equality. Men and boys protested too. Marches may draw attention to an issue better than anything else, and the Selma and Women's Marches are among the most powerful in American history. As much as I believe in protests, the truth of the matter is, I've never been to one, because my parents worry about large crowds and safety issues. We call my dad "the safety officer." If you do participate in a march, it's a good idea to always have an adult with you. While many protests seem safe to me, unexpected things can happen. For example, if the crowd is big,

you could get separated from your parents. Deciding whether marches are right for you should be a decision you make with your caregivers.

In speaking to my friends who've participated in protests, they've told me they are a great way to feel empowered. But if your mom and dad won't let you march, you can follow up with actions like phone calls, petitions, and local government meetings, which will also help lead to change in legislation and policies.

13 POLITICS CAN BE MESSY • Though you may not want my opinion on politics, here it is: I don't like politics. That's not what my work is about at its core. My mission is about the issues of diversity and inclusion. I stay away from choosing between political parties. I focus on the issues. Even when I was interviewing Hillary Clinton, I didn't want to talk to her about politics.

She and I discussed things that were personal. And now that I've given you my opinion, here's some advice to go with it: When you're thinking about your own social action work, try to focus on the issues that you care about. You're taking these steps because you're passionate about walking in the right direction. Focus on the issues that matter to you and the solutions you want to make happen.

14 KNOW THE ROPES AND RISKS • It's super important that protests like sit-ins and marches always be done with supportive adults present. Sometimes, without meaning to, people's passion for a cause can get out of hand and could lead to police action or arrest if they start to engage in what may be considered civil disobedience (a big scary term for when a group is doing something like taking up too much space in a public place, or on a street or sidewalk). For a teenager or group of teens trying to do the right thing, but ends up *over*doing it, an arrest could land you in juvenile detention, and could make it hard to get into college later on. So before you march, stand up by sitting in, or stage a walkout, know the risks. Talk your plan through with adults who are fully aware of what you intend, and are nearby during the protest to help.

For more practical tips to keep you going, and to keep you on the right track, take a peek inside my Activist's Toolbox.

The Activist's Toolbox

21 STAY-STRONG STRATEGIES

7

The Activist's Toolbox

21 STAY-STRONG STRATEGIES

No, not an actual toolbox—it's not like you'll be fixing broken pipes before you go to protest rallies! It's not literal; this toolbox is packed with both the positive thoughts and practical shoes that will keep you happy, sane, safe, on point, and blister-free while you challenge the systems of oppression. Defying the status quo can be an overwhelming task. It's essential to stay calm! (See tip 3.) Before you launch your campaign—whether it is against

> *"Frustration can lead to an innovative and useful idea."*
> —MARLEY DIAS

2 PASSION • You've got to have real feels for your cause. You've got to be fully committed to it. Enthusiasm, like any virus, is contagious. If you're not excited about your cause, how can you expect anyone else to be? But make sure the actions you take are proportionate to what you're trying to achieve. Sometimes just having a simple conversation with someone about your cause can set change in motion.

sexism, environmental destruction, more and healthier options in the cafeteria, or whatever—check out the must-haves on my 21 Stay-Strong Strategies checklist. Then get out there and make some history of your own.

1 A BOOK • Wow, what a surprise that this would be my number one! But seriously, a book (or two, or ten) belongs in your activism toolbox for a couple of reasons: First, you need to be informed. Second, because sometimes, when things get hard, you need an escape to refresh your imagination. A book can be helpful. Read, read, read.

3 SEMI-ZEN JEDI MIND-SET • OK, so passion, fire, the feels, yes. But calmness too. A quiet sense of being. Change can be hard. If it wasn't, all would already be right with the world and we could just kick back in our faux-fur hammocks and swing. Instead, people—in families, school systems, businesses, governments—get fixed in the same old way of doing things, even when it no longer makes sense: When it's obviously discriminatory, bad for the environment, you name it. They'll shrug their shoulders and say, "That's the way it's always been done." They might even suggest that nothing can change. Do not let this get you down! Be ready for it. Just give them your calm smile. And then keep on with your noble mission. Progress can be slow, and slow can be frustrating. Slow can make you want to quit. Or scream. Or quit while screaming. Sometimes

it might feel like two steps forward, one step back. That doesn't mean you're not making progress! Remind yourself of your intention and find calm through the storm. Remember that creating change is a marathon, not a sprint—that there will be obstacles, setbacks, and opponents—then you'll be in a way better headspace to handle disappointments and get back up on your platforms.

4 A PERMIT • To stage or participate in a protest, even when it's peaceful,

you may need a permit. Check with city officials about needing a permit to protest in the places you choose. Each city or district is different and has different laws about how many people can protest and where they can gather. You'll want your protest to be as successful as possible, so get the facts.

5 RESPECT–AND A FIRM HANDSHAKE • Along with passion and Zen, respect completes the vibes trifecta in your toolbox. When you want to correct an injustice so badly that you're willing to put yourself out there to do it, you are quite likely furious about the problem. I was definitely aggravated by the lack of black girl books on my school curriculum, and that frustration motivated me. But being frustrated can be tricky, because if you confront people in a hostile way, even when your anger is completely justified,

it makes them uncomfortable. They get defensive, and they want to get away from you, argue back, and worse yet, not help you change the situation. Worst-case scenario: Actual violence erupts, which, as pointed out earlier, can lead to arrests. That would not be positive for anyone, and doesn't help a worthy cause. It's never a good idea to threaten anyone. In cases like that, you're not only not getting your message across, you're alienating people (there's research about this). And putting yourself at risk too. I'm not saying that in

some situations a certain kind of controlled, collective anger isn't useful—witness all the Women's Marches that took place across the country the day after the presidential inauguration in 2017. But, especially when you're dealing with people like family members or classmates you have to see every single day, it can be more effective to keep it on the positive, no matter what. A firm handshake is a universal way to show respect, to acknowledge the other person as an equal. If a discussion of different opinions starts to turn ugly and you feel yourself escalating into "Hulk smash" mode, take a minute. Breathe. You are not going

> *"Creating change is a marathon, not a sprint."*
> **–MARLEY DIAS**

to change everyone's mind. Not all at once. Not if you call them an ignorant fool straight to their face. By showing respect to others with opposite viewpoints, there's at least a chance you'll plant a seed that just might take root later.

6 A MINI-TRAMPOLINE Further to keeping it on the positive and staying Zen, I, Marley Dias, solemnly swear that it is impossible to stay in a bad mood while hopping up and down. Jumps Against Grumps I say!

7 A PILLOW • Activists need their rest. If you don't sleep you are going to be grumpy and you won't be able to concentrate. A great activist is a well-rested activist.

8 YOUR STORY IN SIXTY SECONDS • The idea is this. If you found yourself in an elevator with someone super important and influential, and you only had those few seconds before the doors opened again to get them to support your goal—a charity run, a food drive,

133

a class trip—what would you say? How could you sum up what you want while still keeping it personal, memorable, intriguing? Elevator pitches are worth developing because they force you to really reflect on your purpose and express it in a "mission statement" (that's sort of a more official term for the same thing, though mission statements are usually longer and in writing, while elevator pitches are out loud and in elevators). For example, that pancake anecdote I told at the very beginning of this book, about white boys and their

dogs? People always remember that. What's your pancake anecdote? Practice it. Record yourself using your phone and time your speech. That way, when you bump into Oprah Winfrey in the snack aisle at the supermarket, you'll be good to go.

9 THE GOOGLE APP • If this is the information age, then Google on your phone, if you have one, means info at your fingertips. That info should include . . .

10 A SOLID NEWS SOURCE • In case this hasn't come up in your current or previous social studies class, a free press is part of the foundation of our democracy. It's also our right as citizens, protected by the First Amendment to the Constitution. Now, I love BuzzFeed with all its listicles and quizzes ("What Would Your Gem

Be in *Steven Universe?*" I must know. Right now!). And cable news can be as melodramatic and opinionated as any reality TV show. But for straightforward reporting of real facts and all sides of an issue, download a newspaper. Most major ones—the *Wall Street Journal*, the *New York Times*, the *Washington Post*, the *Chicago Tribune*, and the *San Francisco Chronicle*, to name just five—have been published since the 1800s. They have a track record you can usually trust. You don't have to get your hands all inky like in ye olden days! Just read one online: Scan the front page for lead stories, every day if you can, and when something grabs your interest, dig deeper. Some sites are free, others offer a limited number of free views per month, and digital subscriptions are not too pricey. An affordable monthly fee is a small price to pay for knowledge. Be well informed.

11 **A FULLY CHARGED PHONE** • And, if you have a phone, a portable charger to go with, if possible. Don't you hate how battery power starts to drain the moment you unplug your phone and head out the door? Argh! Whatever event you're attending—a speech that you might want to record, inspirational music you may want to listen to while you wait, an incident you might want to video—arrive powered up.

12 PAPER AND PEN •
Because tech can fail.
When you can't get
a Wi-Fi signal or your phone
inconveniently dies, or you lose it
(it happens), go old-school. Write
stuff down! In a notebook, save
your experiences, the things that
you hear and see. Always date
your events as well.

13 YOUR POLITICIANS'
PHONE NUMBERS
It's too obvious to
state that you should have your
home phone number and at least
one other emergency contact—a
nearby relative or trusted neigh-
bor—saved in your address book.
Besides that, though, add the
numbers of your elected officials.
Every American citizen is represented by two senators and one
congressperson. Go here to look
yours up—it's so easy: usa.gov/
elected-officials. While you're
at it, check out sites like Count-
able (countable.us) and apps like
5 Calls (5calls.org), which high-
light current events, people to
contact about them, and scripts of
what to say—especially useful for
the conversationally challenged.

"In our high-tech world, the
old-fashioned phone call is still
one of the most important tools
we have as citizen activists," Massachusetts representative Katherine
Clark said in an interview with
Teen Vogue. "It can be one of
the best ways the public has of
asserting pressure . . . You walk

down the hallways [of Congress] and hear the ringing—you can tell something's really on the minds of the public." When an issue concerns you, just call up the office of your senator, congressperson, even the president, and tell them your opinion. Call back if you get a busy signal. Leave a voicemail if you get a recording. Every call is logged (every email too), meaning your voice *literally* counts.

Enjoying a moment with Valerie Jarrett.

14 THE POWER OF SOCIAL MEDIA •

Your phone is charged, you've got Google for searches, newspaper apps for info, and the phone number of the president of the United States on speed dial. Now, if you can gain the support of influential online groups who'll help make your campaign go viral—like I was lucky enough to do with Black Twitter—you'll be golden. By linking your Facebook, Twitter, and Instagram, you can post simultaneously across all platforms, expanding your reach while staying on message. For tips on how I did it, see Chapter 5!

> *"Share your goals and ask for help."*
> —MARLEY DIAS

15 **THE POWER OF TRADITIONAL MEDIA •** The *World* Wide Web (as our parents once called it) is global. And it makes the entire wired planet crazy-interconnected— you can Snapchat with Japan while sitting home in your jammies. But then again, the most effective activism often takes place irl at the local level. I might never have been invited to appear on the *Ellen* show if her producers hadn't seen me profiled in the *PhillyVoice.* Your town's weekly circular, your school newspaper, basic cable, and community college TV stations: These outlets always need new "content"— human interest stories that directly relate to their audience. You're a human! You're interesting! You have a cause everyone in your community should know

SuperGirl Olivia Raymond and I are glad to meet authors Rita Williams-Garcia (left) and Jacqueline Woodson.

about. So while you're waiting for the video of your elevator pitch to blow up on YouTube, start spreading the word through local print, TV, and online interviews. It just might lead you to Trevor Noah one day.

16 THE SUPPORT OF COMMUNITY • A social action project must be social. Hand-in-hand with local media is community involvement. Look for opportunities to invite people to join you.

Also seek out places where people gather and let you talk about your cause: at school assemblies and after-school clubs; at your church, synagogue, or mosque; at community board meetings; at neighborhood block parties. These are all perfect places to get support from people affected by the same issue you're trying to solve. Share your goals and ask for help. Whether you're lobbying for a stop sign at an accident-prone intersection or an organic garden to revive an abandoned lot, there's strength in numbers. And in neighbors and peers. Though if you're having trouble gathering a group to go with you on a march in the middle of winter, then at least bring . . .

17 A BEST FRIEND • Do you remember being assigned a buddy on elementary school field trips? That logic is sound. You had each other's backs! As you're processing everything that's happening around your cause, your ideas and observations need to go somewhere.

What better place than to those who know you best and can handle it? If you can get even one friend involved, not only does that make social activism more fun, it's also very helpful to have someone hold your place while you go to the bathroom after drinking all that . . .

18 WATER • Because shouting "The People. United. Can Never Be Divided!" nonstop, talking to people face-to-face or on the phone can leave you with a dry throat.

Community support is essential.

Friends make activism easier and more fun.

19 A POWER SUIT • Or whatever outfit makes you feel empowered and fierce. For me, it's a suit all the way. It keeps me feeling professional and stylish all the time. If for you it's a purple tutu, that's equally perfect.

20 COMFORTABLE SHOES • Sneakers, most likely. Activism often puts you on your feet—traveling places, waiting patiently for a response, talking to people. With all that standing and waiting, activism demands

comfort. I suggest you get a pair of sneakers that you can wear with a dress or jeans. And fuzzy socks: Ahhhh . . . so cushy. Plus, everyone can relate to them. If you end up in a disagreement, show 'em your socks and watch your differences fade away.

21 DOLLARS • Whether it's to get gum or a quick snack, activism means traveling and you always need some quick cash handy. For those who are involved in marching, you definitely need enough cash to get you back home from wherever it is you're going, just in case.

> *"Put many tools in your toolbox. It gives you more options."* —MARLEY DIAS

How to Read

WHY IT'S MORE THAN WORDS

8

How to Read

WHY IT'S MORE THAN WORDS

I know it may seem weird to have a chapter at this point in the book called "*How* to Read." If your eyes are on this page, then you already know *how to read* (and hopefully you *like* what you're reading).

But I am sure you know that there's so much more to reading books, and loving them, than just looking at the words in front of you.

What's the point of having a lot of books if you're not going to

146

> ## *"Reading is so much more than words on a page."*
> —MARLEY DIAS

READ EVERY DAY

If you want to get good at dancing, tennis, swimming, singing, or any other activity, you need to practice it daily. When I first started learning to play the viola, it was a struggle. My fingers hurt and I got blisters and marks from its strings. And oh, my neck! Trying to balance that instrument properly took some figuring out. But I got better and better

open them, or if reading feels like a chore? This chapter shows you how you can make reading fun. For any parents and teachers who bought this book I've included information that you can use too, delivered straight from an adult who, like you, wants to find ways to help kids love to read.

When reading is easy and enjoyable, it's like being in a smooth-riding car (in my case, this would be a white g-wagon). Books drive you where you want to go. Here are some ways I've found to enjoy reading. But first, like a car, fill your tank with some much-needed fuel. When you put these ideas into practice, you'll be ready to rollll!!

whenever I took my viola out of its case, and spent time playing it a little each day. In time, when I started to be able to play whole songs that made people smile, I wanted to play it more and more. Soon, *wanting* to play and *loving* to play became the same thing.

Reading's like that too. To get good at it, and to learn to love it, you have to do it Monday through Sunday. After a while, reading will put a smile on your face and will fill you up like music.

WRITE EVERY DAY

It's a fact (at least my teachers have told me this), there is a direct connection between becoming a great reader and being able to write well. It makes perfect sense. Think about it. Anyone who's writing a lot is creating words and ideas, and sentences, and paragraphs. If these flow from your pen, they can also leap from the pages of a book in words and ideas, and sentences, and paragraphs that have flowed from the pen or laptop of an author. Writing daily doesn't need to be formal or hard. Just get out a notebook and scribble something—anything you feel like saying is good enough. The main thing is to do it as much as you can. Sometimes I write rhymes, sometimes I write poetry, and sometimes I write down stuff that makes me happy or mad!!

DON'T WAIT FOR LATER

It's easy to promise yourself that you're going to read and write every day, but it can be harder to really stick with it. Sometimes the chorus of "I will do it later" is one of the loudest and most obnoxious groups of voices ever. It's made up of all the chatter in your mind that tells you not to bother with something now because it's too hard, or you're not in the mood, or you have better things to do. But you will not get to it later. Sometimes after I put something off, it never ends up happening. Later is not greater. Use your time now to travel to exotic places, or discover a whole new bunch of facts that make you feel great inside? That's what reading does for you. When you want to put off reading, just say to yourself, now is the best time to be great.

STEP OUT OF YOUR COMFORT ZONE

I can't tell you how many times I've been at a book fair or library and I've heard one kid (we'll call her Caroline) recommend a book to another kid (we'll call her Sylvia), and before Caroline can even put the book in Sylvia's hand, Sylvia says, "No thanks, I don't read fantasy. It's not my thing."

I know it's rude to eavesdrop, and totally not right to crash a conversation, but whenever I hear

> *"Take a moment to look past a book's cover. There may be some gems inside, once you dive into those pages."*
> —MARLEY DIAS

149

these kinds of exchanges, I can't help but just jump in. I used to be this way too, so I really get it. But now I see that reading different types of books is like trying different types of teas. I once said to a girl, "What do you mean, you don't read sci-fi and that it's not really your cup of tea?" Now, you don't know this, but I love Teavana. I have my own teapot and everything. She said, "Have you tried every kind of tea there is, or all kinds of sci-fi books, for that matter?" I see her point. Just like I am trying new types of tea each month, you have to try new types of books.

The point is, before turning your nose up at a reading genre, or category, try it. Even if you don't love it all, stepping out of your reading comfort zone opens your mind, and helps you appreciate the kinds of books that you *do* like even more. If it's a struggle for you to try something new, or to get into a new reading category that you haven't liked in the past, do a genre-swap with a friend. Give her a copy of your favorite work of historical fiction, and ask that she recommend some of her sci-fi favorites. Make a deal that you'll both take a leap out of the "I don't read _____" trap by each reading books recommended by the other.

Rita Williams-Garcia expressing book love.

COVERS REALLY COUNT

When people say you shouldn't judge a book by its cover, what they really mean is that you can't tell how good a book is (in the same way that you can't know the truth about a person) just by looking at the outside.

But it's a fact—lots of people make assumptions based on what they see. This is especially true about book jackets. I've been known to turn my back on a book because its cover doesn't appeal to me right away.

As far as books that feature black girls are concerned, I wish kids had more of a say in what's on the front of a book. There are lots of vibrant covers out there, but there are also some duds.

Hopefully, that's changing, but I wish publishers would realize that black girls, like other kids, appreciate bright colors, just like everyone else (not covers with drab colors), and that we like to see our faces on the fronts of books, rather than pieces of arms and legs and feet.

Even if a book cover isn't the most appealing, it's not that book's fault. Authors don't often have any say in what goes on the covers of their books. The people who work at the publishing company figure that out. (Fortunately, Scholastic, who published this book, and I worked together on its cover, which I think is really great!)

Give every book a chance by picking it up, opening its cover, and reading the flaps to see what the book is about. Then read at least the first three chapters. If they don't grab your attention right away, you can set the book aside and go back to it another time. A few months from now, you may see things a little differently. (Remember what happened with me and *Brown Girl Dreaming*.)

When you find a book that has a winning cover, post about it on social media. It's like sending an Instagram gift to a friend.

READING PICTURES COUNTS

If you're a kid who loves books and stories but struggles with reading, that's OK. Because there's this real thing called "visual literacy" (big term created by adults), which means that you can read the pictures in a book without even looking at the words on the page. That's right, looking at pictures is a form of reading. Picture books are for kids of every age. So if you like books that are filled with pages and pages of watercolors, pen-and-ink drawings, pastels, cartoons, or any other kinds of illustrations, consider yourself somebody who's a kick-butt visual reader. And hey, stack up on graphic novels too, 'cause they're full of images that take

> ## "Books with lots of pictures count!"
> —MARLEY DIAS

you to some of the most amazing places. I love graphic novels and magazines, so I take one with me when I am going places that are going to be loud and will make it hard for me to concentrate on wordy passages.

READ TO ME

Though I read a lot by myself, I still enjoy having a story read to me. If somebody tells you that it's babyish to ask your mom or dad or teacher or friend to read out loud to you, try this. Invite this obviously uninformed person to step over to the nearest bookshelf. Pick up a book and start reading it to them. Read slowly. Really put your heart into it. Then stop abruptly. I bet they will beg you to keep going. ☺

Here's another experiment that has never failed me: No matter what grade you're in, or how old you are, ask your teacher if you can stay for a few minutes after school so that she can read one chapter to you out of your or her favorite book. I bet you she will definitely say yes, because one of the things adults sometimes forget to tell kids is that reading aloud brings them as much happiness as it brings you. And your teacher may even add read-alouds as part of your classroom time.

This same read-aloud love is true of parents. If you ask your mom or dad to read to you for twenty minutes every night, they will jump at the chance, I promise. It's an opportunity to snuggle and parents always love that. You may even be able to sneak in a request for something you really want. If parents or teachers are too busy, read out loud to yourself. News flash (and the big secret some people don't talk about): It's a fact—even the coolest teens like to have stories read to them. I'll be the first to admit it. When somebody reads to me, I totally love it.

Also, reading aloud also helps you become a better reader.

LISTEN!

Audiobooks can also inspire. Imagine hearing awesome actors bring your favorite characters to life. Listening to a chapter each day on your phone can cut school bus rides in half, make long road trips breezy and quick, and keep you company when none of your friends are around.

WATCH OUT FOR THE SUMMER SLIDE

The minute that bell rings at the end of the school year, I'm ready for flip-flops, and I'm super excited to take a break from papers, school-work, and assignments. But here's another fact. And this one comes from real, live scientific studies that show when kids stop reading over the summer, they slip into something called "the summer slide."

It sounds like a ride at a water park, right? But this is a slide of a whole different kind. It's a slippery dip into letting your reading skills drown. When you don't read over the summer, your reading mindset turns to mush and you're not as smart at the start of the next school year. If you haven't opened a book between June and September, it makes doing well in school even harder when you walk into your new classroom in the fall. Your brain will have to work double time to catch up and keep up, so please read over the summer. Please!

TWO-FERS

Books can serve different purposes, which is why I have them stashed all over, and why I'm usually reading more than one book at the same time. Try this: Pick one kind of book for short car trips (like to the grocery store or mall), or to read on the way to school if you ride a bus.

Choose another book for reading in bed at night. Pick a third for any time when you know you'll be waiting and you want the minutes to pass quickly. I usually have one for when I'm in the hair-braiding shop. You can even label your books with the names of where you'll be reading them: Beach. Couch. Bed. Car Trip. Grandma's House.

> *"A love of reading is the most important legacy we can offer to our children."*
> —DR. LAUREN WELLS

HELLO, PARENTS AND TEACHERS (AND ANY ADULT WHO WANTS TO HELP KIDS LOVE TO READ)

Through our work on #1000black-girlbooks and GrassROOTS Community Foundation, my mom and I have met a lot of smart people. Some of them are even over the age of eighteen!

When I was writing this book, it occurred to me that grown-ups might need some help figuring out how to get kids to love reading as much as I do. So I got in touch with my mom's friend Dr. Lauren Wells, former Chief Education Officer for the City of Newark, New Jersey, and asked her what she recommends for parents and teachers.

Like many adults, she couldn't just hand over the goods without first sitting me down to give me a whole bunch of info about why reading is a great idea.

She says a love of reading is the most important legacy grown-ups can offer kids. Reading opens windows to new ideas, people, places, and experiences. Reading also provides mirrors for students to see themselves and their lives reflected in the characters they meet in books, windows for all of us to look into to see cultures other than our own, and doors to enter new worlds.

Dr. Wells was quick to tell me that reading builds vocabulary and background knowledge so that we kids have the tools needed to express ourselves, and to think clearly about our planet and the people who live on it.

Reading gets kids' brains ready for lifelong learning, and develops important skills like stamina, reflection, and empathy. (Can you tell that this doctor knows her stuff?)

My favorite part of what Dr. Wells told me is that reading can be fun, and the more we kids grow to like it, the more we'll want to do it. Amen to that!

Finally, after laying the groundwork for her ideas, Dr. Wells rolled out some really great suggestions for parents and teachers who want to create environments that invite kids to feel confident in reading and to fall in love with stories and books.

PARENTS, THIS ONE'S FOR YOU

• Model reading. Read, read, read to your child, with your child, or in front of your child every day.

• Talk to your child about the books you're reading, and why these make your heart sing. Children pick up cues from parents about what's enjoyable. Put reading high on your "I love to do this" list.

• Immerse your child in books. Transform your entire home into a reading zone by putting books in every room.

• Affirm your child's culture, language, and race by choosing books and stories with characters, places, and experiences that reflect their background.

• Awaken your child to new ideas and experiences in books and stories by asking questions and always answering the questions they have.

• Empower your child by allowing them to choose books to read, whether based on their interests, or on book covers and titles.

• Arm your child by always leaving home with books. When your child gets older, ask if they have a book before leaving for school, the doctor, or a long car ride.

• Cultivate your child's use of language and words. Talk with your child about what's happening in their life and the world around them.

• Build your child's ability to make connections. When you watch television or movies, make connections to characters or ideas in books you have read together.

• Expand your child's reading beyond fiction. Children have great curiosity about plants, animals, people, and events taking place in the world. It's never too early to expose them to historical fiction or nonfiction books.

• Advocate for lesson plans, partnerships, books, and resources for classrooms and schools that are culturally relevant and responsive.

TEACHERS, LISTEN UP

• Immerse school culture in book talks; a few ways to do this are over the intercom, in book clubs, in social media chats, and in school-wide read-alouds.

• Talk about books with the same enthusiasm expressed for joyous experiences, such as sports, video games, action parks, and music.

• Affirm your students' cultures, languages, and races by integrating into the curriculum books and stories with characters, places, and experiences that reflect their backgrounds.

• Awaken students as participants in their own learning

by having them create reading goals for themselves. For example, minutes of reading, numbers of chapters read, reading new genres.

• Empower students by allowing them to pick the books they want to read. Arm your students with the power of their own language and stories by providing them with multiple ways to make personal connections to the texts they read.

• Cultivate independent reading by creating comfortable reading spaces throughout schools. Classrooms, cafeterias, libraries, and cozy nooks in hallways are all fair game.

• Build classroom libraries of interesting, appropriate, and relevant titles.

• Expand reading beyond fiction. Students have great curiosity about plants, animals, people, and events taking place in the world. Use historical fiction or nonfiction books as tools to capture this interest.

• Advocate for curriculum development, partnerships, books, and resources for classrooms and schools that reflect a range of cultures and experiences.

So there it is, from an expert who knows what it takes to make books and kids a winning combination!

Finding the Goods

BYE-BYE, HIDE-AND-SEEK

9

Finding the Goods

BYE-BYE, HIDE-AND-SEEK

Hide-and-seek is a fun game, until it isn't. When I launched #1000black-girlbooks, it was sort of like trying to find something that shouldn't have been hiding. Why were so many books buried and hard to get our hands on?

As soon as the floodgates opened, and I started receiving books from every corner of the world, there was no mistaking the power in the numbers of books I received.

As my mission continues to grow, I'm learning that there are many ways, and lots of good people, who can point me in the right direction when I'm looking for a book. Here's to the end of hide-and-seek.

LOVE THOSE LIBRARIANS

I used to think librarians were little old ladies with bun hairdos and cat-eye glasses. And while lots of librarians are bookish and do tie up their hair, librarians are also some of the wokest people ever. Lots of them do wear glasses. But hey, I do too. In getting to know more and more librarians,

> *"Books are often hidden in plain sight—you just have to look."*
> —MARLEY DIAS

I've discovered that many have entire wardrobes of funky fashion-forward glasses just like I do. That makes a lot of sense. Since librarians and I both do a lot of reading, we need to see clearly. Thank goodness for librarians. They can be super-helpful partners in finding books my friends and I like. That's why I've made it my business to get to know my local branch librarian and the librarian at my school.

And I've let *them* get to know *me* and my family, so they can recommend books. How many times have I told a librarian that I'm looking for a book about _____, but I can't remember

FIVE BOOK-FIND HOT SPOTS

Ready, set, read! Here are some solid sources for getting your hands on great books featuring characters of color.

THE BROWN BOOKSHELF

Brown is beautiful! The Brown Bookshelf promotes awareness of the work of black authors writing for children. Check out their "28 Days Later" initiative that highlights the best books by black creators. Check it out: thebrownbookshelf.com

WE NEED DIVERSE BOOKS

What's in a name? In the case of We Need Diverse Books (WNDB), the name says it all! The WNDB mission is to "put more books featuring diverse characters into the hands of all children." Their vision is to have "a world in which all children can see themselves in the pages of a book." Oh, what a world that would be. To learn more, visit: weneeddiversebooks.org

CHILDREN'S BOOK COUNCIL (CBC) DIVERSITY

Get the insider scoop on what publishers are doing to promote diversity, right in their own offices and among their group of editors, book designers, and even the people who market and sell books. And when you go to college and think you might want to work at a publishing company, the Children's Book Council can open the door to internships. Here's the info: cbcdiversity.com

THE AFRICAN AMERICAN CHILDREN'S BOOK PROJECT AND BOOK FAIR

If you're looking for *the* biggest African American children's book fair in America, this is the go-to spot. The African American Children's Book Project, which focuses on promoting and preserving children's books, hosts "the largest and most longstanding single-day literary event for African American children in the world." If you want to come face-to-face with your favorite authors and illustrators, this is a great place for book fans. Plan your visit to Philadelphia at: aalbc.com/events/african_american _childrens-book-fair.html

COLORING BOOKS

Here's a specially selected list of books for children and teens by diverse authors. This site allows you to write in to tell your own book-finding stories and to make book recommendations. Coloring Books lets you do that. Enjoy! coloringbookslit.com

the full title, or the author's name hasn't stuck? A great librarian can

"**Librarians are the wokest people ever!**" —MARLEY DIAS

take my "I sorta know" description of a book, and nab it quickly. (I always think librarians should go on *Jeopardy!* and win in a bazillion categories).

Librarians spend a lot of time helping lots of different kinds of people, so they know their stuff. Call on them when a book emergency strikes, when you gotta have *that one special book or you need a recommendation to become inspired.*

BOOK FAIRS + BOOK CLUBS = BOOK FUN

It's one thing to have your parents or teachers or a librarian tell you which books they think you'll like, but it's great when you can pick your own book! No doubt—I'm always open to book suggestions, but in the same

TRAILBLAZING LADY

Way before I hatched my plan to find black girl books, there was an amazing librarian bringing her call to the cause. Augusta Baker was an influential children's librarian back in the 1930s at the New York Public Library's 135th Street Branch in Harlem. Just like me, Augusta had once been a girl with a dream. Her hope was to see and celebrate more stories where black girls played important roles. Back then, there weren't nearly as many books with black characters published for young people, but Augusta helped begin to change that with her public storytelling. For every book that wasn't available featuring a black girl, lady Augusta told it like it was by *speaking* stories, some that sprang from her imagination, others that were from the works of the Harlem Renaissance authors who were popular at that time, writers whose books we still read now— Zora Neale Hurston, Jessie Redmon Fauset, Langston Hughes, and Nella Larsen. Like so many pioneers, Augusta was a "first" in many ways, most notably as the first African American librarian to hold a prominent position in the Children's Services department of the New York Public Library. If Augusta were alive today, you can best believe that her tweets would be trending along on Twitter. Because when Augusta Baker spoke, people listened and then spoke up as the result of her passion for kids and books.

Augusta Baker was a history-maker.

BIG-DEAL VIP

The Library of Congress is a huge building in Washington, DC, not far from the White House, where millions of books line the shelves. It's like a castle. The librarian who oversees the Library of Congress is appointed by government officials. When they name the person who will become the Librarian of Congress, it's a Big Deal, because the job is a VIP—a Very Important Position.

Can you believe that for more than two hundred years, the Very Important Position was filled only by white men? Times are changing. In 2016, Dr. Carla Diane Hayden was appointed as the 14th Librarian of Congress. She was the first woman and the first African American to hold the post.

Fortune magazine ranked her as one of the World's 50 Greatest Leaders. She's been leading the charge for more diversity in books for kids. And she's been making some important strides. Looking forward to meeting her soon!

ways that I browse for glasses and sneakers that are *me*, I like to take my time and look for books that speak to my soul.

I've noticed that when *I* pick out my own books, I jump into them more quickly, and I have fun passing them on to friends, because I can tell them this is one I nabbed on my own.

This is where book fairs, catalogs, and online sources can help you choose. Whenever there's a book fair at my school or local community center, people are excited to see what's available. It's like a happy birthday party. As soon as the doors open, book

> ## "Make information free for all."
> —DR. CARLA HAYDEN,
> LIBRARIAN OF CONGRESS

lovers like me, and their families, are all about filling their wish lists by shopping the fair. A librarian in my town helped me find my first reading series, and that's how I got really hooked on libraries.

The same is true for reading clubs that have catalogs and flyers, or online ways to search and select. It's as much fun as checking out the sales at your favorite store. And the books are often available in paperback, so they're affordable.

Find out if your school participates in a book fair or with a reading club provider, or if they're involved with other reading initiatives. If they're not, start one of your own. There are many companies that offer school book fairs. The main thing is getting your hands on great books! ☺

THE COOLEST CLUB EVER

In doing research for this book, I learned that librarians have their own club. And it's one of the coolest clubs to join (if you're a librarian). It's called the American Library Association, aka, ALA.

These are the women and men who select the books that win the major children's literature prizes, such as the Newbery, Caldecott, Coretta Scott King, and Pura Belpré medals. They also choose ALA Notable Books and videos.

Every winter you can tune in to a live press conference where the best books for young people are announced, via live stream. The authors I spoke to told me that it is one of the most exciting, nail-biting moments in the children's literature world.

It's when, for several categories of books, the world waits to hear the answer to . . . "and the winner is . . ." To learn more, check them out: ala.org

Book Talking

SEEING IS BELIEVING

10

Book Talking

SEEING IS BELIEVING

Sometimes the most obvious things aren't always obvious to everybody. When I was launching #1000blackgirlbooks I wanted to get my hands on as many books with black women and girls as protagonists as I could find. And I wanted to collect books that were fun to read and presented black girls in the best possible light. Also, lots of these books, but not all, were written by black authors.

But in starting my book-finding charge, it didn't take long

> *"A great book can stand the test of time. If you love it, read it again and again. It'll never go out of style."*
> —MARLEY DIAS

to figure out that while there were so many amazing books with black girls front and center—that were written by super-smart and talented authors—these weren't obvious to everyone. I'm pretty sure that's because so many black girl books aren't being placed in visible spots in bookstores and public libraries, or being assigned in schools and classrooms. Books with black girls in the starring role are often put in the background. They just haven't been celebrated as much as other kinds of books. Even now, people wonder, *How many books starring black girls can there*

really be? I've even asked myself that question.

But guess what? I soon found out that's like asking *How many stars can there be in the sky?* There are SO MANY stars out there. SO MANY! But sometimes you have to look hard to find them. Because they can be hiding among the clouds. Or, maybe they're covered up by smog or pollution. Clouds, smog, and pollution are similar to when people have doubt that something amazing is possible—they block the light! But at the same time, stars and the sun and the moon

are always shining, even when we can't see them. Even when they may be covered up.

The overwhelming support for my #1000blackgirlbooks campaign proved there are lots of books with black girls in them, and people do know about them! There are tons of titles. I learned that these books shine brightest when the clouds of doubt and negativity clear away.

As much as I like science classes (and smart-girl glasses), I'm not an expert on constellations and planets. But I do know that a telescope can help you see stuff that you may not have noticed before. And a telescope can make things that seem far away look much bigger, closer, brighter, and more real.

So OK, this is not rocket science. I figured out that books need "telescopes"—something to bring them into better view—if they want to get noticed. And nobody has to go to some big astronomy supply superstore to bring books into focus. Here are some ways we can all help black girl books (or anything you're passionate about) get their shine, starting right now, this minute.

> *"Books are like stars! No matter what color the characters are, they deserve to shine!"*
> —MARLEY DIAS

BOOK TALKING

You know when you hear that expression, "Everybody's talking about _____"? And that makes you want to hurry up and see what the buzz is about? This same idea can be applied to your favorite books.

Book talking is when you tell everybody you know about books you love. But there's more to it than just telling them the titles of books. Book talking also involves selling them on how awesome a book is by giving details about the characters in the story, what happens to the girl in chapter one that makes you want to keep reading, and how the book makes you feel when you read it. Just be careful not to reveal too much about how the book ends. Spoilers can hurt your favorite book's chances of getting picked up. I've seen some people who will avoid reading a book if they know how it ends.

So, when you book talk, leave the ending wide open. *Talk, talk, talk* about everything leading up to . . . that moment when you say, "But to find out what happens after her best friend moves away, and her life gets crazy when the class snake ends up in the picnic basket, and she wishes her friend, who loves snakes, was there to help, but isn't . . . *read the book*!"

KEEP IT SHORT

Like a movie trailer or television commercial, video yourself giving a book talk. Book talks should be short, and they should pack a lot of punch. It's hard to believe, but most commercials are only thirty seconds to two minutes long. Book-talk videos can be a bit longer, but keep your on-air time focused and engaging. You wouldn't want your viewer to lose interest. You want it to be short enough to go on Instagram or Snapchat, and then you can put it on your story. (If you don't have a social media account, send your video to your friend either through email or text.) By making it engaging, people can watch it, then go about the rest of their day and still remember what they saw in your video.

SHARE YOUR TRAILER

It's like they say—sharing is caring. And in the case of a book talk, spreading the love lets people know how much you care about the books you read, and how important reading and books are to you. And so, once your book-talk video is done, share it with friends, classmates, family, teachers, and anyone who may also like what's between those pages you love. You can even stage a "book-talk video reveal" by hosting a party to premiere your video, and asking others to bring their book talks to share as well, either delivered live or onscreen. Everyone can bring their books, swap them, and agree to pass them on to others. Don't forget popcorn. Or, if you come over to the home of the DiasCrew, get ready for breakfast at dinnertime, or sushi rolls any time of the day or night!

SHARE THE PLOT—AND THE LOVE

Briefly explain the who, what, when, and where of the book. Outline the plot—the beginning, middle, and sort-of end, though not enough to give the end away. Then, tell your viewers why you love the book! Did it make you laugh or cry—or cry from laughing? Did the dialogue and characters fill your heart and mind with new feelings and ideas? If you've read other books by the same author, you can reference them and recommend those too. Ask your teacher if you can start each class with a book talk. Even better, ask your principal if you can do a short book talk over the loudspeaker in the morning as part of your school's announcements.

READ A PASSAGE

This is your moment to give viewers a true taste of your book's flavor. Pick one of your favorite sections and read it. If you like acting, you can really bring it on by using the voice of the main character or narrating with feeling. If you are really feeling it, try wearing something that speaks to the book's theme. (Did someone say "leopard print"?)

RATE THE BOOK

On a scale of 1 to 5 stars, how many stars would you give this one? If the book is less than glistening, be kind and constructive in your comments. If the book is over-the-top amazing, gush from here to eternity. Remember that ratings are based on your own impressions of the book. Others may have different opinions.

TRUE SUPERSTAR STORY

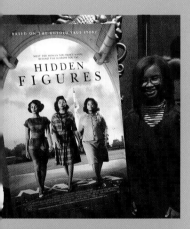

Here's an example of when real life is as glistening as fiction. Speaking of stars and the wide-open galaxy of black girl talent, the book *Hidden Figures* by Margot Lee Shetterly highlights three powerhouse black female mathematicians who worked at NASA in 1961 and helped the United States in the Space Race with the Soviet Union.

With pencils, paper, and brainpower, they calculated flight trajectories for several space missions. Translation: Thanks to Mary Jackson, Katherine Johnson, and Dorothy Vaughan, rocket ships were successfully launched into space and returned safely.

These ladies advanced science and math to such a degree, they've been referred to as "the math machines," and they've been named national heroes. The book *Hidden Figures* became a bestseller, one of the hottest teen reads, and a major motion picture starring Janelle Monáe as Mary Jackson, Taraji P. Henson as Katherine Johnson, and Octavia Spencer as Dorothy Vaughan.

Getting It Done

TODAY, TOMORROW, ALWAYS

11

Proud to be with (left to right) Mom, Valerie Jarrett, Linda Sarsour, Donna Lieberman, Anne Delaney

Getting It Done

TODAY, TOMORROW, ALWAYS

OK, I admit it, I love words. I love cool words, and "dynamic" is one of them. But wait. Before I start in on "dynamic," let me tell you something else. As I was starting to use this word more and more, I had to say to myself, "Marley, you can love all the words you want, but it's a good idea to know what a word truly means—and what you're actually saying when you use the word."

And so, I looked up "dynamic"

in an online dictionary (thank you, Merriam-Webster, for coming through loud and clear on my phone).

What I found was this definition: "Dynamic: an underlying cause of change."

Think about it. "Underlying" means all the support and help you may not see, but that's totally needed to keep things flowing.

So, the dynamics of getting it done—today, tomorrow, always—are about having feet firmly planted in the present, while setting your intentions for the future and moving toward your purpose one step at a time.

"I know that I'm definitely not the only kid out there who wants to make big changes. We're all in this together."
—MARLEY DIAS

GETTING-IT-DONE DYNAMICS

Ruby Bridges said it best: "Don't follow the path. Go where there is no path, and begin the trail. When you start a new trail equipped with courage, strength, and conviction, the only thing that can stop you is you!"

I can only imagine what Ruby must have had to endure as she created a path as the first black child to desegregate the all-white William Frantz Elementary School in New Orleans, on November 14,

1960. Ruby was an activist at age six. She had to put up with people shouting hateful words, standing in her way, and throwing tomatoes on the freshly pressed dresses her mom gave her to wear each day. At times, people even threatened her life. But she never gave up.

Thanks to Ruby and others like her, all kinds of people can work and play and live together today. And black kids and white kids can go to the same school. I'm thankful for that. I see my mission as an extension of what Ruby and other activists successfully accomplished to help promote racial harmony and progress.

Working toward change can be hard sometimes, but you just have to keep moving forward, like Ruby did. And sometimes you have to say no, and not budge from your conviction. When it

Ruby Bridges was brave, strong, and serious about getting it done.

all starts to feel hard and scary, I try to remember these very simple slogans to keep me going.

REMEMBER THE POWER OF "WE"

There's tons of strength in numbers. When working toward any goal, gather your friends and family to support you for the ride, walk, or talk. Independence is a great quality, but when you're trying to make big changes, interdependence is better. More gets you more.

DON'T GIVE UP WHEN IT GETS HARD . . . WAIT FOR IT

Sometimes you want to back down or abandon your mission, especially when it seems that nothing much is happening to move it forward, or when you're meeting resistance. But hang in there. A breakthrough might be right around the corner. If you fold too soon, you'll miss it.

BEGIN WHERE YOU ARE

Look down right now at where you're standing. This is where you can start to make your dreams come true—in this moment. Today.

KEEP IT SIMPLE

I'm all about big plans and ideas, but I try not to complicate things. I keep a notebook where I write down super-simple actions I can take each day—concrete activities that are doable.

LISTEN TO LEARN, LEARN TO LISTEN

As a kid who's often dealing with grown-ups, I can be quick to state my opinions and ideas, because I want to be heard. Let's face it, adults sometimes know better, so it's easy to be eager to hurry up and make your point. But sometimes I need to listen too. Because the best ideas can come by hearing what somebody else has to say.

THE FUTURE IS FRIENDLY

Please don't waste time obsessing or worrying about what might or might not happen. Stay on course, focus your heart, soul, and mind on what *needs* to happen, and trust that everything will work out. Things may not come to pass in ways you expect, but believing that whatever the future holds will be good is at the core of important work. All things are for the good.

Whew! What a journey! And believe it or not, I'm just getting started. I never dreamed that a pancake breakfast with my mom would turn into an all-out movement that's putting books into the hands of kids everywhere, and showing people that black girls' stories are important, fun, worthy, universal, and can stand the test of time. And that our stories can become classics. And that books with black girls as main

STAY IN GRATITUDE

There are two words that can clear away almost any roadblock: *thank you*. Remember to use these words often and mean them. Say them to everyone who supports your cause. You can even whisper *thank you* under your breath when some ignorant person stands in your way. They're to be thanked too for showing you how not to be.

characters appeal to all kinds of kids (even those who mostly like dog books). And that narratives told in black girls' voices can be included among the best of the best in literature for young people. And, just as important, that books with black girls on the covers—shown full-on, with eyes, lips, noses, and hair and entire bodies—are beautiful and to be celebrated.

Speaking of beautiful black people to celebrate, Viola Davis, the Academy Award–winning actress (and also one of the few black women to nab that golden Oscar statue!), once said in an interview that if you're afraid of diving into something, then just dive into it afraid.

Probably everyone feels "afraid to dive" at some time or another. I mean, is it really fun to throw yourself from a high-up place, not fully knowing what's below? But at the same time, the unknown can be an awesome adventure that can take you to incredible new places.

I've learned there are always people to catch you, to help you, and to show you how to "swim" once you've landed in what might be unknown waters.

People often ask me, "Marley, since you've now collected so many books, and have exceeded your original goal, what's your *new* goal?"

The truth of the matter is, I don't yet have a *new* goal, but I do have a bigger idea, now that, with the help and support of so many people, we've done what we originally set out to do. Note that I say *"we've"* done this. Embracing the collective "we" is an important part of how anything meaningful gets accomplished. (And it's the reason it's my A #1 "Getting-It-Done Dynamic.")

My bigger, higher, get-it-done dream is that *we* (all people, everywhere, who care about compassionate social action) have

entire school districts assigning books that are very diverse. I'm also excited to find ways that lesson plans and school boards can come together to make books with characters of different races, gender identities, and abilities required reading. This is one of the big get-it-done dreams I'm eager to achieve. But I can only do these important things with the help of my friends and family, and others who want to make a difference—including you.

The title of this book is very special to me. I thought a long time about *Marley Dias Gets It Done: And So Can You!*

When I wasn't finishing up homework, or studying for a test, I took almost every free moment I had writing in my notebook about the message I want to share with readers.

My parents and I spent hours talking through all the parts and pieces of this book. The title was something we debated and discussed over many dinners.

The word "done" seems kind of final. But when you put it together with "*gets* it done," it reminds me that "getting" is something that continues.

In my case, "getting" means taking the first steps into a brand-new day. It means waking up and smelling the pancakes that will inspire and nourish us for what's ahead.

It means getting woke.

Getting together.

Getting support.

Getting heard.

Getting results.

And getting also involves *giving*—it isn't always about getting what you want, but working toward helping others get what *they* need. If there's one thing I've learned, it's that you can't get or keep anything of value unless you give it away through generosity and service.

The way I see it, "getting it done" is about who you are, what you stand for, and how you treat people in the process of making changes happen.

In many books, when you come to the end of the last chapter, it says "the end." But for me, my mission is an exciting new adventure that's at the very beginning—today, tomorrow, always.

I'm just getting started!

And so can you.

Right now.

Acknowledgments

I have a lot of things to be grateful for. In no particular order, I would love to thank the following for the contributions they have made to my life.

Mommy: Mommy, I love you so much and thank you for just giving me the world. As much as I may be stubborn, I will always try my best to make you proud. You have taught me everything I know, and have guided me to show my truth. I just love you and you make me smile. From taking me to get my nails done to helping me prepare for events like InBound and United State of Women, you give your all to help me. Thank you.

Dad: Dad, you are awesome and I love you. You cheer me up on sad days and take me to do fun things and teach me lots and lots. You come through in the clutch to help me with whatever I need. The tricks you have up your sleeves you have passed on to me to help make me a better person. Thank you for making me such a creative, humorous, and resourceful person.

SuperGirls: Thank you so much for loving and appreciating me. I love all of you so much. Your raw energy, talent, and gigantic hearts make me happy every day. I wish the best for you forever and always. Use the principles to guide you so that you can show your full beauty and potential. Take the resources GrassROOTS has provided you too and use them to make you flourish.

The Fergus Family: Tori, Mr. Troy, Ms. Sonya, and Troy. You all are a fantastic family who have dedicated so much time to helping me succeed. Thank you. You are all generous, kind, and thoughtful. I wish the best for all of you in whatever you do.

The Raymond Family: Olivia, Ms. Sherille, Mr. Ronald, Kai, and Reese. Thank you for helping me all the time. You have given so much to me and to the campaign. You are a model family who give your hearts to everything.

The Anekwe-Barnett Family: Amina, Ms. Lisa, Ms. Patrice, and Ms. Coops. You as a family are a web of wonder. You are extremely openhearted and gifted people. I thank you for staying with me no matter what and bringing cooked food and energy to every party.

Skai Blue Media: Ms. Rakia, Ms. Lisa, Major Almaz, Ms. Christana, Mr. Javier, Ms. Leah, Ms. Jordan. Thank you for helping me spread my message. Without all of you, my beliefs and ideas wouldn't be able to reach the world. Because of you the world is learning daily about the importance of diversity. Thank you, Ms. Rakia, Ms. Lisa, and Major Almaz, especially, for personally taking the time to help me succeed.

Ava DuVernay: Thank you, Ms. Ava. Thank you for choosing to invest in black girls when it wasn't the popular choice. You are creating the next generation of leaders.

Book Team: Thank you so much to Andrea Davis Pinkney, Charlotte Sheedy, Mary Claire Cruz, Abby Dening, Lauren Donovan, Erin O'Connor, Maya Frank-Levine, Bonnie Cutler, Natalia Remis, Siobhan McGowan, and Elizabeth Parisi for helping me make this masterpiece. Thanks also to Kristen Harper, EdM, Senior Policy Specialist, Child Trends; and Deborah Temkin, MA, PhD, Program Area Director, Education Research, Child Trends, for their careful reading of my manuscript's references to social media safety and protest guideline safety.

Your hard work and trust in me are gifts I could never pay back. I just am so appreciative of the opportunities you have given to me.

Elle.com Team: Ms. Mattie, Ms. Leah, Ms. Nikki, Ms. Julie, Ms. Chloe, Ms. Gina, Ms. Kristina, Ms. Chaedria, Dr. Melissa, and Mr. Joe. I am so thankful for the chance you took on me to make something wonderful. You have created much space for my imagination to roam free and for me to feel limitless.

My Teachers at St. Cloud Elementary: Thank you to all of my teachers from elementary school. Ms. Danzig, Ms. Wert, Ms. Clark, Mrs. Berkowitz, Mrs. Stoner, and Mr. Frank have all helped to lay a foundation for me to be who I am today. You supported my wit, intelligence, and humor. You made me smile every day and made learning fun and engaging. Thank you for the experiences. Those six years went by too fast.

My Roosevelt Friends: "Welp" (as we call ourselves) is one of the most incredible groups of young women I have met. Anna, Delia, Camille, Lizzie, Lucy, Ruby, Oona, Maria, Tori, Fernanda, Nia, you all are astonishingly beautiful, smart, talented, and fabulous people. As I met all of you, I was welcomed with open arms and invited to join you all as friends. I hope we all can stay friends past middle school and continue to grow as young women. No matter what, you will always be my Wams and Wummies (a nickname) and I appreciate you.

Jacqueline Woodson and Rita Williams-Garcia: Thank you for taking me under your literary wings and allowing me to learn from your ways. Thank you for coming to my elementary school and blessing my peers with your fantastic words. The knowledge you have spread in the world is so valuable and I thank you every day for helping me. You helped me carve out more crazy summers and you help me dream.

The Martin Family: Ms. Carol, Mr. Josh, Caila, and Cydni. Thank you for motivating me to get out there, do new things, and be my best self for the world to see. Your experience and knowledge taught me and your jokes gave me comfort. Thank you for welcoming me.

The Stricker-Coughlin Family: Thank you, Auntie Mary, Uncle Dave, Alice, and Ruby for being there for me always. No matter what, I can trust you to be there for me. My second first family.

Other Special People:

Charlotte: Thank you for believing in my possibilities.

The Vega-Olds Family: Titi, your gift started it all.

Aunty Iya: Thank you for helping me find my way.

Jacsyn and Alli Scott: Thank you for letting me be creative and teaching me to experience joy.

Ariyan Wint and Tenisha Malcolm: I love you both. You sweat love.

Nana Monica: You always make me smile.

Grammy: Your creativity helped Daddy help me.

The Bohm-Jackson Family: Because of you I will always have Che and Rena, great clothes, and food made fresh.

Ms. Aja and Kindred the Family Soul: You opened the door for me and shared me with the world.

Erin Young: It's fair enough to say that you are great.

Lillian Jones: I love you.

Kent: You are the best/worst babysitter. Thanks.

Tina Tchen, Valerie Jarrett, and the White House Counsel on Women and Girls: You are the absolute symbol of girls' possibilities.

Warby Parker: Thanks for creating a space for me.

African Health Now and Nana Eyeson: Because of you I had a life-changing experience.

Beverly Bond: Thank you for honoring me and my work.

The Ellen DeGeneres Show: So grateful to everyone who supported me. This show changed my life forever.

Heben and Tracy from *Another Round*: So imaginary and so real.

Hillary Clinton: I will remember to resist and persist.

WBGO Radio: Thanks for choosing me before anyone else did.

PhillyVoice: Thanks so much for telling my story.

Lily Eskelsen Garcia: Thank you for your high energy and confidence in me.

Grace Mahary: Beauty and brains in one.

Angela, the Best Tour Guide of Disney World: My first and best experience ever.

Larry Wilmore: Sorry I have to tell the world that you are a big softie. You are so nice.

Franchesca Leigh: Thank you for being so witty.

Chloe and Halle: My sisters.

Phoebe Robinson: Thank you for choosing to support me.

CBS This Morning: You made television fun when I was really, really scared.

Mikaila Ulmer: I look up to you.

Monique Coleman: Thank you for creating a pathway for all of us.

Jamaica Gilmer: You are the best!

Andrea Cipriani Mecchi: Thanks for always making me feel and look beautiful.

Elaine Welterworth: Thank you for your support.

Finally, thanks to all of you who chose to donate books, and to the many schools and communities who opened their doors and hearts to me and my message.

1000 Is My Lucky Number

When it comes to books that feature black girls as main characters, the more we have, the more we can share. That's why I've put together my own Black Girl Books Resource Guide. This free resource guide was created as a result of the #1000blackgirlbooks campaign. The guide includes books that were donated during the initial stages of my campaign, and that have been cataloged into an easy-to-use database. Here, I've included about 500 titles, focusing on books for middle graders and young adults.

What's here is a sampling of books from the full assortment of donated titles. This is not meant to be a comprehensive guide; there is more work to be done.

The information listed in the complete guide includes books for all ages and some for adults. The guide is appropriate for youth, parents, educators, schools, and libraries. It currently lists more than 1000 unique book titles, and is always evolving. The entire guide is available for download at: grassrootscommunityfoundation.org/ 1000-black-girl-books-resource-guide

INDEPENDENT READER

BOOK AUTHOR	BOOK TITLE
A.A. Riley	Introducing Sophia Firecracker
Adrian Fogelin	Crossing Jordan
Adrienne Vincent Sutton	Bad Hair Day
Alan Schroeder	Baby Flo: Florence Mills Lights Up the Stage
Alan Schroeder	In Her Hands: The Story of Sculptor Augusta Savage
Alexander McCall Smith	The Great Cake Mystery: Precious Ramotswe's Very First Case
Alexander McCall Smith	The Mystery of Meerkat Hill: A Precious Ramotswe Mystery for Young Readers
Alexander McCall Smith	The Mystery of the Missing Lion: A Precious Ramotswe Mystery for Young Readers
Alexandra Duncan	Sound
Alice Childress	Rainbow Jordan
Alice Randall	The Diary of B.B. Bright Possible Princess
Alika Turner	June Peters, You Will Change the World One Day
Alvin Silverstein	Can You See the Chalkboard?
Amy Reeder, Brandon Montclare	Moon Girl and Devil Dinosaur
Andre Norton	Lavender-Green Magic (The Magic Books #5)
Andrea Davis Pinkney	Bird in a Box
Andrea Davis Pinkney	The Red Pencil
Andrea Davis Pinkney	Abraham Lincoln: Letters From a Slave Girl (Dear Mr. President)
Andrea Davis Pinkney	Let It Shine: Stories of Black Women Freedom Fighters

BOOK AUTHOR	BOOK TITLE
Andrea Davis Pinkney	Raven in a Dove House
Angela Johnson	A Cool Midnight
Angela Johnson	Heaven
Ann Cameron	Gloria Rising
Ann Cameron	Gloria's Way
Ann E. Burg	Serafina's Promise
Ann M. Martin	Jessi's Secret Language (The Baby-Sitters Club #16)
Ann Rinaldi	Hang a Thousand Trees With Ribbons: The Story of Phillis Wheatley
Ann Rinaldi	Taking Liberty: The Story of Oney Judge, George Washington's Runaway Slave
Anna McQuinn	Lola Loves Stories
Antoinette Lawrence, Terry Lewis	I Remember
Antonia Harlan	Hello, My Name Is Josie Mae Bricker
Atinuke	Hooray for Anna Hibiscus! (Anna Hibiscus Book #2)
Atinuke	Good Luck Anna Hibiscus! (Anna Hibiscus Book #3)
Atinuke	Have Fun Anna Hibiscus! (Anna Hibiscus Book #4)
Barbara Bazaldua	The Princess and the Frog: Tiana's Dream
Barbara E. Barber	Saturday at the New You
Ben Hatke	Little Robot
Berlie Doherty	The Girl Who Saw Lions

Bette Greene	Philip Hall Likes Me. I Reckon Maybe	Christopher Paul Curtis	The Mighty Miss Malone
Beverley Naidoo	Journey to Jo'burg: A South African Story	Coleen Murtagh Paratore	Sunny Holidays
B.J. Barratt	Angel Bear	Connie Rose Porter	Meet Addy: An American Girl (An American Girl: Addy #1)
Blue Balliett	Hold Fast	Connie Rose Porter	Addy Learns a Lesson: A School Story (An American Girl: Addy #2)
Bonnie J. Glover	The Middle Sister	Connie Rose Porter	Addy's Surprise: A Christmas Story (An American Girl: Addy #3)
Brenda Wilkinson	Ludell	Connie Rose Porter	Happy Birthday, Addy!: A Springtime Story (An American Girl: Addy #4)
Brenda Woods	The Blossoming Universe of Violet Diamond	Connie Rose Porter	Addy Saves the Day: A Summer Story (An American Girl: Addy #5)
Brigitte White	All-American	Connie Rose Porter	Changes for Addy: A Winter Story (An American Girl: Addy #6)
Bud Kliment	Billie Holiday (Black Americans of Achievement)	Crystal Allen	The Magnificent Mya: Tibbs Spirit Week Showdown
Camille Yarbrough	Tamika and the Wisdom Rings	Crystal Allen	The Laura Line
Candy Dawson Boyd	Circle of Gold	Dasia "DasiaVu" Edmond	Uniquely Made: "Girls Don't Play Football"
Carole Boston Weatherford	Voice of Freedom: Fannie Lou Hamer: The Spirit of the Civil Rights Movement	Dawn C. Gill Thomas	Kai: A Mission for Her Village, Africa, 1440 (Girlhood Journeys Collection)
Caroline Pignat	The Gospel Truth	Debbi Chocolate	NEATE to the Rescue (NEATE 1)
Cat Winters	The Steep and Thorny Way	Debbi Chocolate	Elizabeth's Wish (NEATE 2)
Catherine Egan	Shade & Sorceress (The Last Days of Tian Di Book 1)	Delandria Mills	Demi's Flute: Entering the Realm of Sound
Catherine Egan	The Unmaking (The Last Days of Tian Di Book 2)	Delia Sherman	The Freedom Maze
Catherine Egan	Bone, Fog, Ash & Star (The Last Days of Tian Di Book 3)	Denise Lewis Patrick	A New Beginning: My Journey with Addy (American Girl Beforever Series: Addy)
Chandra Sparks Taylor	The Greatest Gift of All	Denise Lewis Patrick	Meet Cécile (American Girl Series)
Cheryl Mullenbach	Double Victory: How African American Women Broke Race and Gender Barriers to Help Win World War II	Denise Lewis Patrick	No Ordinary Sound (American Girl Beforever Series: Melody #1)
Christopher Grant	Teenie	Derrick Barnes	Ruby and the Booker Boys #1: Brand-New School, Brave New Ruby
Christopher Paul Curtis	Elijah of Buxton	Derrick Barnes	Ruby and the Booker Boys #2: Trivia Queen, 3rd Grade Supreme

Diana G. Gallagher	Monica and the Bratty Stepsister
Diana G. Gallagher	Monica and the Crushworthy Cowboy
Diana G. Gallagher	Monica and the Doomed Dance
Diana G. Gallagher	Monica and the School Spirit Meltdown
Diana G. Gallagher	Monica and the Sweetest Song
Diana G. Gallagher	Monica and the Unbeatable Bet
Diana G. Gallagher	Monica and the Weekend of Drama
Diana G. Gallagher	Monica and the Worst Horse Ever
Diana G. Gallagher	Haunted Love (Claudia and Monica: Freshman Girls)
Diana G. Gallagher	Tested
Dianne Ochiltree	Molly, by Golly!: The Legend of Molly Williams, America's First Female Firefighter
Dorothy Sterling	Mary Jane
Douglas Brinkley	Rosa Parks: A Life
Dream Jordan	Hot Girl
Earl Sewell	Myself and I
Eleanora E. Tate	Just an Overnight Guest
Eleanora E. Tate	Celeste's Harlem Renaissance
Eleanora E. Tate	Thank You, Dr. Martin Luther King, Jr.!
Eleanora E. Tate	The Minstrel's Melody (American Girl History Mystery)
Eleanora E. Tate	The Secret of Gumbo Grove
Elizabeth D. Gray	Becoming Me: Journal Affirmations for Girls Vol 2
Elizabeth D. Gray	I Am Enough: Journal Affirmations for Girls
Elizabeth D. Gray	I Am Beautiful: Journal Affirmations for Girls
Elizabeth Fitzgerald Howard	Aunt Flossie's Hats (and Crab Cakes Later)
Ellen Labrecque	Who Was Maya Angelou?
Ellen Levine	Henry's Freedom Box: A True Story from the Underground Railroad
Eloise Greenfield	Sister
Eloise Greenfield	In the Land of Words: New and Selected Poems
Eloise Greenfield	Koya Delaney and the Good Girl Blues
Emma L. Price	Portia's Incredible Journey
Enigma Alberti	Spy on History Mary Bowser and the Civil War Spy Ring
Ermila Moodley	Path to My African Eyes
Esme Raji Codell	Sahara Special
Esme Raji Codell	Vive La Paris
Evelyn Coleman	White Socks Only
Evelyn Coleman	Shadows on Society Hill: An Addy Mystery (American Girl Mysteries Series)
Franck Prévot	Wangari Maathai: The Woman Who Planted Millions of Trees
Franklyn Branley	The Moon Seems to Change
Freddi Williams Evans	A Bus of Our Own
G. Willow Wilson	Vixen: Return of the Lion
Gabrielle Douglas, Michelle Burford	Grace, Gold & Glory: My Leap of Faith
Gloria Respress-Churchwell	Robert Churchwell: Writing News, Making History: A Savannah Green Story

Gwen Everett	Li'l Sis and Uncle Willie		Jacqueline Woodson	I Hadn't Meant to Tell You This
H. Chuku Lee	Beauty and the Beast		Jacqueline Woodson	Lena
Hilary McKay	Lulu and the Rabbit Next Door		Jacqueline Woodson	Hush
Hilary McKay	Lulu and the Hedgehog in the Rain		Jake Maddox	Softball Surprise
Hope Anita Smith	Mother Poems		Jake Maddox	Cheer Challenge
Ida Siegal	Big News! (Emma Is on the Air #1)		Jamaica Kincaid	Annie John
Ida Siegal	Party Drama! (Emma Is on the Air #2)		Jamilah Tetterton	From Where Do We Come?: Revisiting Our Past While Paving the Way Forward
Ida Siegal	Showtime! (Emma Is on the Air #3)		Jana Laiz	A Free Woman on God's Earth: The True Story of Elizabeth Mumbet Freeman, the Slave Who Won Her Freedom
Ifeoma Onyefulu	A Is for Africa		Jane Sutcliffe	Marian Anderson
Imani A. Alsobrook	Maya in the Middle		Jane Yolen	Miz Berlin Walks
Irene Latham	Leaving Gee's Bend		Janet McDonald	Twist and Turns
J.L. Powers	This Thing Called the Future		Jayne Cortez	Coagulations: New and Selected Poems
Jacqueline Woodson	Between Madison and Palmetto		Jen Cullerton Johnson	Seeds of Change: Wangari's Gift to the World
Jacqueline Woodson	Last Summer with Maizon		Jenny Lombard	Drita, My Homegirl
Jacqueline Woodson	The House You Pass on the Way		Jeremy Whitley	Save Yourself (Princeless 1)
Jacqueline Woodson	From the Notebooks of Melanin Sun		Jeremy Whitley	Get Over Yourself (Princeless 2)
Jacqueline Woodson	The Dear One		Jeremy Whitley	The Pirate Princess (Princeless 3)
Jacqueline Woodson	Brown Girl Dreaming		Jeri Watts	Kizzy Ann Stamps
Jacqueline Woodson	Feathers		J.N. Childress	The Briefcase of Juris P. Prudence
Jacqueline Woodson	Locomotion		Jewell Parker Rhodes	Bayou Magic
Jacqueline Woodson	Behind You		Jewell Parker Rhodes	Towers Falling

Jewell Parker Rhodes	Ninth Ward
Jim Starlin	The Infinity Gauntlet
Jo Whittemore	Confidentially Yours #1: Brooke's Not-So-Perfect Plan
Jo Whittemore	Confidentially Yours #2: Vanessa's Fashion Face-Off
Joan M. Lexau	Striped Ice Cream
Josh Farrar	A Song for Bijou
Joyce Annette Barnes	The Baby Grand, the Moon in July, and Me
Joyce Carol Thomas	The Gospel Cinderella
Joyce Hansen	Yellow Bird and Me (163 Street Trilogy)
Joyce Hansen	The Gift-Giver (163 Street Trilogy)
Joyce Hansen	I Thought My Soul Would Rise and Fly: The Diary of Patsy, a Freed Girl, Mars Bluff, South Carolina, 1865 (Dear America)
Juanita Havill	Jamaica's Blue Marker
Juanita Havill	Jamaica and Brianna
Justin Scott Parr	Sage Carrington: Eighth Grade Science Sleuth
Justine Larbalestier	Liar
K.A. Applegate	The Secret (Animorphs #9)
Kajara N. Nebthet	I Get Energy from the Sun
Karen Deans	Swing Sisters: The Story of the International Sweethearts of Rhythm
Karen English	Wedding Drama (Nikki and Deja)
Karen Hesse	Witness
Kate Hannigan	Cupcake Cousins, Book 1: Cupcake Cousins

Kate Hannigan	Cupcake Cousins, Book 2: Summer Showers
Kate Messner	Rescue on the Oregon Trail (Ranger in Time #1)
Kathleen Duey	Zellie Blake: Lowell, Massachusetts, 1834 (American Diaries Series)
Kathleen Kudlinski	Harriet Tubman (History's All-Stars)
Kathryn Lasky	Vision of Beauty: The Story of Sarah Breedlove Walker
Kathryn Lasky	A Voice of Her Own: The Story of Phillis Wheatley, Slave Poet
Kekla Magoon	Shadows of Sherwood: A Robyn Hoodlum Adventure
Kekla Magoon	Fire in the Streets
Khara J. Campbell	Island Girl
Kristen Larsen	Lily's Pesky Plant
Kristin Earhart	Race the Wild #1: Rain Forest Relay
Kristin Hunter Lattany	The Soul Brothers and Sister Lou
Kristin Levine	The Lions of Little Rock
LaNiyah Bailey	Not Fat Because I Wanna Be
Laurie Halse Anderson	Forge
Leah Bassoff, Laura DeLuca	Lost Girl Found
Lee-Ling Ho	Samsui Girl
Linda Lowery	Aunt Clara Brown: Official Pioneer
Linda Sue Park	A Long Walk to Water
Louise Borden, Mary Kay Kroeger	Fly High!: The Story of Bessie Coleman
Louise Fitzhugh	Nobody's Family Is Going to Change

Lucille Clifton	The Lucky Stone	Meg Cabot	From the Notebooks of a Middle School Princess
Lucy Jane Bledsoe	Cougar Canyon	Megan Stine	Who Is Michelle Obama?
Lynda Blackmon Lowery	Turning 15 on the Road to Freedom: My Story of the 1965 Selma Voting Rights March	Merle Hodge	For the Life of Laetitia
M. Mitnsi	The Homework Mystery	Michael J. Rosen	Elijah's Angel: A Story for Chanukah and Christmas
Mabel E. Singletary	Something to Jump About (The Double Dutch Club Series)	Michael Scotto	Latasha and the Little Red Tornado
Mabel E. Singletary	A Promise and a Rainbow (The Double Dutch Club Series)	Michaela DePrince	Ballerina Dreams: From Orphan to Dancer
Macqueline Woods	Swag Diaries: Students with A+ Grades Swag 4 Life	Michaela DePrince	Taking Flight: From War Orphan to Star Ballerina
Marc Sumerak	Ororo: Before the Storm	Michaela MacColl, Rosemary Nichols	Freedom's Price
Margaret Musgrove	The Spider Weaver: A Legend of Kente Cloth	Micheline Hess	Malice in Ovenland Vol. 1
Marie Bradby	Some Friend	Michelle M. Spady	Kiana S.M.A.R.T. for Class President
Mariko Tamaki	This One Summer	Mildred D. Taylor	Roll of Thunder, Hear My Cry
Marilyn Hilton	Full Cicada Moon	Mildred D. Taylor	Song of the Trees
Marilyn Levy	Run for Your Life	Mildred D. Taylor	Let the Circle Be Unbroken
Marilyn Nelson	How I Discovered Poetry	Mildred D. Taylor	The Gold Cadillac
Marilyn Nelson and Tonya C. Hegamin	Pemba's Song: A Ghost Story	Milton J. Davis	Amber and the Hidden City
Marti Dumas	Jala and the Wolves	Monica Edinger	Africa Is My Home: A Child of the Amistad
Mary Ann Rodman	Yankee Girl	Nancy Farmer	A Girl Named Disaster
Mary Hoffman	Starring Grace	Nancy Farmer	The Eye, the Ear and the Arm
Mary Hoffman	Encore, Grace!	Natasha Trethewey	Native Guard: Poems
Mary Hoffman	Bravo, Grace!	Nichole M. Nunes	Short Hair Is Awesome Too!
Mary Hoffman	Princess Grace	Nikki Giovanni	Cotton Candy on a Rainy Day

Nikki Grimes	Meet Danitra Brown		Patricia Hermes	Summer Secrets
Nikki Grimes	Danitra Brown, Class Clown		Patricia Hruby Powell	Josephine: The Dazzling Life of Josephine Baker
Nikki Grimes	Halfway to Perfect (A Dyamonde Daniel Book)		Patrick S. Muhammad	Little Librarian Girl
Nikki Grimes	Almost Zero (A Dyamonde Daniel Book)		Phillip Hoose	Claudette Colvin: Twice Toward Justice
Nikki Grimes	Rich (A Dyamonde Daniel Book)		Phyllis Robinson	Wishing on a New Moon
Nikki Grimes	The Road to Paris		Quentin Holmes	Real Street Kidz: Chasing Action
Nikki Grimes	Planet Middle School		R.J. Williams	Adventures of Alleykats: Historical Sleuths: The Missing President (Volume 1)
Nikki Grimes	Jazmin's Notebook		R.L. Omer	The Prince and Timberance
Nikki Grimes	Talkin' About Bessie: The Story of Aviator Elizabeth Coleman		Rachel R. Russell	Dork Diaries
Nnedi Okorafor	Binti		Raquel Hunter	Diary of a Diva's Daughter with a DO-IT-ALL Dad starring Brave Rave (Diary of Brave Rave Volume 1)
Nnedi Okorafor	Akata Witch		Rebecca Hayes	Private Cathay's Secret
Nnendi Okorafor-Mbachu	Zahrah the Windseeker		Renee Skelton	Harriet Tubman: A Woman of Courage
Ntozake Shange	Ellington Was Not a Street		Renée Watson	What Momma Left Me
O.T. Begho	The Adventure of Obi and Titi: The Hidden Temple of Ogiso (Volume 1)		Richard Corman	Misty Copeland: Power and Grace
Patricia C. McKissack	A Picture of Freedom: The Diary of Clotee, a Slave Girl, Belmont Plantation, Virginia, 1859 (Dear America)		Rita Williams-Garcia	Gone Crazy in Alabama
Patricia C. McKissack	Color Me Dark: The Diary of Nellie Lee Love, the Great Migration North (Dear America)		Rita Williams-Garcia	One Crazy Summer
Patricia C. McKissack	Nzingha: Warrior Queen of Matamba, Angola, Africa, 1595 (Royal Diaries)		Rita Williams-Garcia	Jumped
Patricia C. McKissack	Sojourner Truth: Ain't I a Woman?		Rita Williams-Garcia	Like Sisters on the Homefront
Patricia C. McKissack	Goin' Someplace Special		Rita Williams-Garcia	Blue Tights
Patricia & Fredrick McKissack	Miami Jackson Sees It Through		Robert D. San Souci	The Talking Eggs
			Robert D. San Souci	Cendrillon: A Caribbean Cinderella

Robert Munsch	Makeup Mess	Shelley Tougas	Little Rock Girl 1957: How a Photograph Changed the Fight for Integration
Robin Russell	Summer Island: A Prince in Peril	Shereece Connolly-McLeish	The Adventures of Ajalon & Kayla: The Emerald Globe
Rod Martinez	Cassie's Curse: Death at Cobra Lake	Sherri Graves Smith	Is My Cup Empty?
Rosa Guy	The Friends	Sherri L. Smith	Hot, Sour, Salty, Sweet
Rosa Parks	Dear Mrs. Parks: A Dialogue with Today's Youth	Sherri L. Smith	Sparrow
Ruby Bridges	Through My Eyes	Sherri L. Smith	Flygirl
Ruby Bridges	Ruby Bridges Goes to School: My True Story	Sherri L. Smith	Orleans
Ruth A. Rouff	Ida B. Wells: A Woman of Courage	Sherri Winston	President of the Whole Fifth Grade
Sandra Belton	Ernestine & Amanda	Sherri Winston	President of the Whole Sixth Grade
Sandra Belton	Summer Camp: Ready or Not! (Ernestine & Amanda)	Stephanie Perry Moore	True Friends (Carmen Browne series #1)
Sarah Mlynowski, Lauren Myracle, Emily Jenkins	Upside Down Magic	Stephanie Perry Moore	Sweet Honesty (Carmen Browne series #2)
Scott O'Dell	My Name Is Not Angelica	Stephanie Perry Moore	Golden Spirit (Carmen Browne series #3)
Shannon Hitchcock	Ruby Lee & Me	Sundaira Morninghouse	Habari Gani? What's the News? A Kwanzaa Story
Sharon M. Draper	Stella by Starlight	Sundee T. Frazier	The Other Half of My Heart
Sharon M. Draper	Copper Sun	Sundee T. Frazier	Cleo Edison Oliver, Playground Millionaire
Sharon M. Draper	The Birthday Storm (Sassy #2)	Susan E. Goodman	The First Step: How One Girl Put Segregation on Trial
Sharon M. Draper	The Silver Secret (Sassy #3)	Sylviane A. Diouf	Bintou's Braids
Sharon M. Draper	Double Dutch	Tamora Pierce	Daja's Book (Circle of Magic, No. 3)
Shelia P. Moses	The Sittin' Up	Tamora Pierce	Magic Steps (The Circle Opens book 1)
Shelia P. Moses	Sallie Gal and the Wall-a-Kee Man	Tanita S. Davis	Happy Families
Shellie Moss	Najah's Quest: The Adventure Begins	Tanita S. Davis	Mare's War

Tanita S. Davis	Peas and Carrots		Una LaMarche	Don't Fail Me Now
Tanya N. Ragbeer	The Journeys of Tati		Valerie Wilson Wesley	Willimena Rules: 9 Steps to the Best, Worst, Greatest Holiday Ever!
Tee Michelle	The Adventures of Lil Tonya		Victoria Bond and T. R. Simon	Zora and Me
Tee Michelle	Lil Tonya & A.J.'s Summer (The Adventures of Lil Tonya)		Victoria Garrett Jones	Marian Anderson: A Voice Uplifted
Tee Michelle	Lil Tonya Visits Kindergarten (The Adventures of Lil Tonya)		Virginia Hamilton	Cousins
Tee Michelle	Lil Tonya Presents Whole Name, Long Vowels, Nickname, Short Vowels		Virginia Hamilton	Bluish
Teleah Scott-Williams	Brother		Virginia Hamilton	Sweet Whispers, Brother Rush
Teresa Reed	Keisha Leads the Way		Virginia Kroll	Masai and I
Teresa Reed	Three Cheers for Keisha		Walter Dean Myers	At Her Majesty's Request: An African Princess in Victorian England
Terra Elan McVoy	This Is All Your Fault, Cassie Parker		Whoopi Goldberg	Sugar Plum Ballerinas: Sugar Plums to the Rescue
Tiffany Nicole Smith	Delaney Joy: Fairy Exterminator (Fairylicious #2)		Winifred Conkling	Passenger on the Pearl: The True Story of Emily Edmonson's Flight From Slavery
Tonya Bolden	Finding Family		Yolda Zeldis McDonough	What Was the Underground Railroad?
Tonya Bolden	Searching for Sarah Rector: The Richest Black Girl in America		Yona Zeldis McDonough	Who Was Harriet Tubman?
Tonya Cherie Hegamin	Willow		Yona Zeldis McDonough	Who Was Sojourner Truth?
Tonya Ellis	Sophie Washington: The Snitch		Yvonne S. Thornton, M.D.	The Ditchdigger's Daughters
Tori Kosara	Gabby Douglas: Going for Gold		Zora Neale Hurston	The Six Fools
Tracey Baptiste	The Jumbies			
Tracey West	Home: The Chapter Book			
Traci L. Jones	Finding My Place			
Traci L. Jones	Standing Against the Wind			
Tui T. Sutherland	Against the Tide (Spirit Animals, book #5)			

YOUNG ADULT READER

BOOK AUTHOR	BOOK TITLE	BOOK AUTHOR	BOOK TITLE
Allison Whittenberg	Sweet Thang	Celeste O. Norfleet	Pushing Pause (Kenisha Lewis #1)
Amir Abrams	Caught Up	Celeste O. Norfleet	Fast Forward (Kenisha Lewis #2)
Angela Johnson	The First Part Last	Celeste O. Norfleet	Getting Played (Kenisha Lewis #3)
Anita Silvey	The Essential Guide to Children's Books and Their Creators	Celeste O. Norfleet	Download Drama (Kenisha Lewis #4)
Anne Schraff	Wildflower	Celeste O. Norfleet	She Said, She Said
Anne Schraff	Until We Meet Again	Chaka Khan	The Chaka Khan Song Book: Piano/Vocal/Guitar
April Randolph	Tasha and KK	Charles Sullivan	Children of Promise: African-American Literature and Art for Young People
April Randolph	Following Tasha (Tasha and KK)	Chimamanda Ngozi Adichie	Purple Hibiscus
Audre Lorde	Zami: A New Spelling of My Name: A Biomythography	Constance Burris	Black Beauty
Babygirl Daniels	Glitter	Dawn Prough	City of Promise
Ballou High School Writers	How to Grow Up Like Me: The Ballou Story Project (Volume 1)	Dia Reeves	Slice of Cherry
Barbara J. Rebbeck	Nola Gals	Dia Reeves	Bleeding Violet
Brandy Colbert	Pointe	Diana G. Gallagher	Homecoming (Claudia & Monica: Freshman Girls)
Brittany Baker	The Season of Autumn: Nothing Lasts Forever (Seasons)	Diana G. Gallagher	New Firsts (Claudia & Monica: Freshman Girls)
Calvin Slater	Hold Me Down (Coleman High #2)	Earl Sewell	Decision Time (A Keysha and Friends Novel)
Calvin Slater	Game On (Coleman High #3)	Earl Sewell	Lesson Learned (A Keysha and Friends Novel)
Carla Shedd	Unequal City: Race, Schools, and Perceptions of Injustice	Earl Sewell	Maya's Choice (A Keysha and Friends Novel)
Carole Boston Weatherford	Becoming Billie Holiday	Evelyn Fairbanks	The Days of Rondo
Carole Ione	Pride of Family: Four Generations of American Women of Color	Farai Chideya	The Color of Our Future: Race in the 21st Century

Felicia Pride, Debbie Rigaud, Karen Valentine	Hallway Diaries: How to Be Down/Double Act/The Summer She Learned to Dance
Greg Pak	Storm Vol. 2: Bring the Thunder
Hannah Moskowitz	Not Otherwise Specified
Harriet Ann Jacobs	Incidents in the Life of a Slave Girl
Heidi W. Durrow	The Girl Who Fell from the Sky
Jaclyn Dolamore	Magic Under Stone
Jacqueline Thomas	Simply Divine
Jamie Reed	Living Violet (The Cambion Chronicles #1)
Jamie Reed	Fading Amber (The Cambion Chronicles #3)
Jayde Brooks	Daughter of Gods and Shadows
Jennifer Latham	Scarlett Undercover
Jewell Parker Rhodes	Ninth Ward
Jewell Parker Rhodes	Sugar
Joan R. Sherman, ed.	African-American Poetry: An Anthology, 1773-1927
Joan Steinau Lester	Black, White, Other: In Search of Nina Armstrong
Karen Sandler	Awakening (Tankborn Series #2)
Karen Sandler	Rebellion (Tankborn Series #3)
Keith Lee Johnson	Little Black Girl Lost
Kelli London	Boyfriend Season
Kelli London	Uptown Dreams
Kimberly Reid	Perfect Liars
Kimberly Reid	Sweet 16 to Life (Langdon Prep #3)
L.J. Willson	Snitch
Lamar Giles	Endangered
Laura Rose Wagner	Hold Tight, Don't Let Go: A Novel of Haiti
Leslie McGill	The Game
Martha Southgate	The Taste of Salt
Maya Angelou	Maya Angelou: Poems
Maya Angelou	Wouldn't Take Nothing for My Journey Now
Maya Angelou	And Still I Rise
Mia McKenzie	The Summer We Got Free
Michelle Lynch	A Girl You Know
Monica McKayhan	Jaded
Nalo Hopkinson	The Chaos
Ni-Ni Simone	Teenage Love Affair
Ni-Ni Simone	Down by Law (Throwback Diaries #1)
Ni-Ni Simone	True Story (Ni-Ni Girl Chronicles Book 1)
Ni-Ni Simone	Upgrade U
Ni-Ni Simone	Get Ready for War (Hollywood High book 2)
Ni-Ni Simone	Put Your Diamonds Up (Hollywood High book 3)
Ni-Ni Simone	Lights, Love & Lip Gloss (Hollywood High book 4)
Ni-Ni Simone, Kelli London	The Break-Up Diaries: Vol. 1

Nikki Carter	Step to This (So For Real #1)	ReShonda Tate Billingsley	Real As It Gets (Rumor Central, book 3)
Nikki Carter	It Is What It Is (So For Real #2)	Rita Williams-Garcia	P.S. Be Eleven
Nikki Carter	It's All Good (So For Real #3)	Ronne Hartfield	Another Way Home: The Tangled Roots of Race in One Chicago Family
Nikki Carter	Cool Like That (So For Real #4)	Rosa Guy	My Love, My Love, or The Peasant Girl
Nikki Carter	Doing My Own Thing (Fab Life)	Rosa Guy	Ruby
Nikki Carter	Get Over It (Fab Life)	Sapphire	Push
Nikki Carter	On the Flip Side (Fab Life)	Sharon M. Draper	Darkness Before Dawn
Nikki Carter	Time to Shine (Fab Life)	Stephanie Perry Moore	Keep Jumping / No Hating (Cheer Drama / Baller Swag) (Lockwood High Series) (Lockwood Lions)
Nikki Carter, Kevin Elliott	The Break-Up Diaries: Vol. 2	Rosalie T. Turner	Freedom Bound
Nikki Giovanni	Bicycles: Love Poems	Terry Farish	The Good Braider
Nikki Grimes	A Girl Named Mister	Theresa Cameron	Foster Care Odyssey: A Black Girl's Story
Noni Carter	Good Fortune	Tia Williams	It Chicks
P.J. Converse	Subway Girl	Veronica Chambers	Mama's Girl
Paula Chase	Flipping the Script (Del Rio Bay Clique #5)	Victoria Christopher Murray	Diamond (The Divas)
Phillip Thomas Duck	Dirty South	Victoria Christopher Murray	Veronique (The Divas)
Ray O'Conor	She Called Him Raymond: A True Story of Love, Loss, Faith and Healing	Victoria Christopher Murray	India (The Divas)
Renée Watson	This Side of Home	Walter Dean Myers	Crystal
ReShonda Tate Billingsley	Nothing But Drama (Good Girlz, book 1)	Zetta Elliott	A Wish After Midnight
ReShonda Tate Billingsley	Getting Even (Good Girlz, book 4)	Zetta Elliott	The Door at the Crossroads
ReShonda Tate Billingsley	Rumor Central		
ReShonda Tate Billingsley	You Don't Know Me Like That (Rumor Central, book 2)		

PHOTO CREDITS

About the Author

MARLEY DIAS is the remarkable teenage social activist who launched the #1000blackgirlbooks campaign, an international movement to collect and donate children's books that feature black girls as lead characters. With the help of the GrassROOTS Community Foundation (GCF), Marley leveraged the power of social media to reach a large audience. Soon her story went viral and was picked up by media outlets around the globe, as well as bloggers, schools, youth-focused organizations, and thousands of individuals who wanted to participate in the project. Today, Marley has become one of the most high-profile young leaders in the world. She is a sought-after speaker, writer, and media presence who has appeared on *The Nightly Show*, *Today*, *CBS This Morning*, *The Ellen DeGeneres Show*, and many more television outlets. Marley has been featured in the *New York Times*, has been recognized as a "21 under 21" ambassador for *Teen Vogue*, and is an editor-in-residence for Elle.com. She also launched a national literacy tour in partnership with the White House during the Obama administration. She lives in New Jersey with her mother and father.